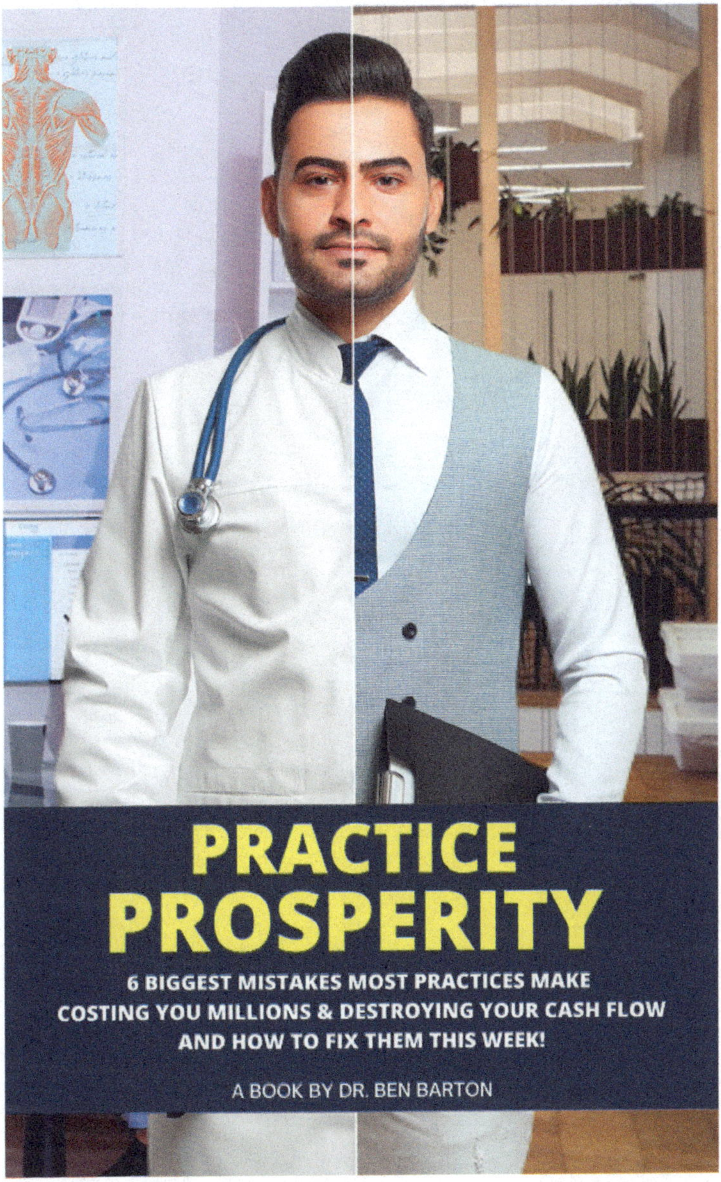
PRACTICE
PROSPERITY
6 BIGGEST MISTAKES MOST PRACTICES MAKE
COSTING YOU MILLIONS & DESTROYING YOUR CASH FLOW
AND HOW TO FIX THEM THIS WEEK!
A BOOK BY DR. BEN BARTON

Practice Prosperity

The Six Biggest Mistakes Most Practices Make Costing YOU Millions & Destroying Your Cash Flow and How to Fix Them This Week

By
Ben Barton D.C.

Copyright 2023

Copyright 2023 Ben Barton D.C.
ISBN: **9798861929073**

All rights Reserved. No part of this book may be reproduced, stored in a retrieval system or transmitted in any form or by any means without the prior written permission of the publisher.

Disclaimer: The information contained in this book on healthcare management and business development (the "Book") is provided for general informational purposes only. It is not intended as legal, financial, or professional advice, and should not be relied upon as such.

The author and publisher of this Book have made reasonable efforts to ensure that the content is accurate and up to date at the time of publication. However, they make no representations or warranties of any kind, express or implied, about the completeness, accuracy, reliability, suitability, or availability of the information, products, services, or related graphics contained in the Book for any purpose.

The information presented in this Book should not be considered a substitute for professional advice or consultation. Readers are encouraged to seek the advice of qualified professionals regarding specific healthcare management and business development issues. The author and publisher disclaim any liability for any loss or damage arising from reliance on the information provided in this Book.

Furthermore, the mention of any specific healthcare management strategies, business models, or case studies in this Book does not constitute an endorsement or recommendation by the author or publisher. Readers should conduct their own research and due diligence before implementing any practices described in the Book. The author and publisher shall not be held responsible for any direct, indirect, consequential, or incidental damages or losses arising out of the use of the information contained in this Book. Any reliance you place on the information presented in this Book is strictly at your own risk.

The author and publisher are not responsible for any actions taken based on the information provided. The inclusion of any external links or references in this Book does not imply endorsement or approval of the linked websites, their operators, or their content. The author and publisher have no control over the nature, content, and availability of those sites. Every effort has been made to respect copyrights and intellectual property rights. If any copyright infringement has occurred inadvertently, the author and publisher will rectify it upon notification. By reading this Book, you acknowledge and agree to the terms and conditions of this disclaimer.

The author will not be responsible for any piss poor results from the use of this information and systems. Victimhood mentality and fear will prevent you from being successful with these systems so for your sake and your family's, check those at the door and leave them behind.

This book is dedicated to Christian, Jordyn and Heather, my loving family who put up with WAY more than they should with my career. Thank you for being supportive and allowing me the time to write this on weekends. Heather, thank you for being my biggest supporter and helping with the editing. My grammar is atrocious so technically you wrote half this book. I definitely could not have done it without you.

I also have to give a very special thanks to Dr. Dean Banks. He was my editor-in-chief and I cannot tell you how many times he emailed me with a piece of the book and the question, "what in the hell are you talking about here"?? Dean has been extremely successful in the medical space and his time and expertise have been invaluable in the creation of this book. Dean, I appreciate you.

I am also forever grateful to my home group The Heritage and the Sober Mafia in my hometown, Mt. Pleasant. Through their love and support over the past six years I have been able to live a life of peace that I never could have imagined in my drinking days. You are all my family and I love you all dearly.

ALL proceeds from my books go to the newly formed Upward Bound Kids Foundation, which I started in late 2022. This non-profit organization will provide leadership scholarships to the children and teenagers of parents who have died from alcohol and drug addiction. We will work in tandem with the Apogee Strong foundation to deliver these programs to at-risk youths whose lives have been impacted by this horrible disease. This effort and support of this initiative is something I am extremely proud of and will launch in the summer of 2023. Service work has become my passion, and my own struggle with alcoholism and subsequent recovery drove me to set up this organization as a way to support the children of those who weren't able to find the recovery that I am so very grateful to have.

Testimonials

I am thrilled to express my deep admiration for Dr. Ben Barton and his remarkable contributions to business owners , and entrepreneurs in the medical industry. His exceptional business acumen, combined with his unparalleled communication skills, has been a beacon of clarity for business owners, entrepreneurs and investors within the medical field. His unwavering dedication to helping individuals navigate the intricacies of the medical landscape is truly commendable. Through his expertise, countless professionals have found renewed certainty and direction in their pursuit. Making him an invaluable asset to the medical community.

Sean Briscombe- Author, The Truth About Taxes. Austin Texas

I have worked off and on with Dr. Barton over the past 11 years. His knowledge base and ability to ramp up service verticals quickly is incredibly valuable. I have earned millions of dollars based on his strategies and help. I highly recommend and cannot thank Dr. Barton enough for his support.
Dr. Mark Luckie DC Charleston Testosterone Charleston South Carolina

Dr. Barton's understanding of marketing and the sales cycle is second to none. He is incredibly proficient at teaching these principles to me and my staff. I am grateful I have had him in my corner both professionally and as a mentor.
Dr. Paul Constante DC Dynamic Chiropractic Louisville Kentucky

Dr. Barton has been a wonderful guide to me in my practice, particularly when I decided to open up a mens

health and hormone center. He was instrumental in helping me make the correct decisions on floor plans, marketing and also implementing systems. I cannot explain in words how much he has helped me over the past two years.
Dr. Mark Isben MD. Helena Montana.

Dr Barton is one of the best clients I have even worked with. He has single handedly made me millions. Just stop whatever it is you're doing and follow his lead.
Nate Leadholm Max Effect Marketing. Denver Colorado

Table Of Contents

Introduction

Chapter 1.
Cash Flow Killer Mistake Number 1: Not Having a Detailed Phone Tracking, Recording and Auditing System

Chapter 2
Cash Flow Killer Mistake 2: Not Understanding the Sales Cycle and the Inability to Convert Expensive Leads

Bonus 1: The Easiest Referral System Ever!

Bonus 2: Handling Objections (This one training is worth an extra 25k a month in your office!)

Bonus 3: Role Play Training

Chapter 3.

Cash Flow Killer Mistake 3: Not Having a Detailed Marketing Plan, and How it is Costing You Millions

Chapter 4.
Cash Flow Killer Mistake 4:
Not Keeping Track of and Understanding the Importance of Statistics

Chapter 5.
Cash Flow Killer Mistake 5:
Not Understanding the Difference Between Being Busy and Being Productive, and Why it is So Important

Bonus: Gameday: How a Productive Way Should Look

Chapter 6.
Cash Flow Killer Mistake 6:
Not having a Detailed Follow Up System for Old Leads. Patients and Video Testimonials. Amateurs vs. Professionals

Conclusion

Appendix A

Appendix B

Introduction

After being in practice for over 20 years and consulting for the past four, I have seen specific patterns that almost every clinic in the country faces week by week, month by month, and year by year.

No matter how many staff they do or don't have, how much revenue they generate, how much money they spend on advertising, no matter what new machine they just spent a fortune on that the sales rep promises will generate millions, they all seem to have the exact same challenges. This book addresses the six really simple mistakes I see being made by almost every business owner in practice and how to fix them QUICKLY. Some of you will read this book and say, "I can see your point here," or "I need to add that in." Maybe you see the systems here and say, "I already do that system," or "My problems lie elsewhere in staff issues." You might say, "This is too basic to be valuable." Well, that is the point. Within these pages, you will learn the most significant and most straightforward fixes that will deliver the biggest impact on bottom-line systems that you can implement immediately (immediately, meaning like this week) to start to scale your business.

Even after working with hundreds of clinics across the country, it always amazes me how less than 10 percent even get the phones right. It is sad to walk into an office that has been told they just need to "market more," and that will solve their problems, only to see the owner go broke and inaccurately think their problem is that the marketing is not working or their competition is too strong. Neither is valid. Marketing always works. Some forms are better than others, but it all works. The only competition you have is yourself and your own limiting beliefs, as well as the lack of the correct systems that could turn things around and have a massive impact on your bottom line.

I want to introduce one of the most important principles I learned in the book Atomic Habits. The book by James Clear discusses the role of goal setting and how goals are important but without proper habits or processes in place these goals are most often not obtained. This philosophy is 100 percent accurate and also directly tied to what we will cover in this book. You can make goals all day long. Your goals can be big, small, yearly, weekly, and even daily, but none matter. The systems and processes we put in place lead to long-term success. Right now, you probably think this dude has lost his damn mind. Every winner I know sets goals and focuses on them! Without goals, we have no road map to get where we are going! Yeah, I get that. (See mistake number 3.) I am not saying you don't need to set targets and goals. Of course, you do. I am saying that focusing on building good processes is more effective than solely fixating on the end result. By creating systems and processes that support our desired goals, we increase the likelihood of achieving our goals exponentially. It does not matter how high or, unfortunately, how low you set your goals because you will never reach or hit that goal consistently without processes in place since *we always fall back to the level of our systems.* It is more important that we focus on mastering processes and improving our processes if we want to reach our goals. Particularly the systems that automate our time, level up the patient experience and make them feel at home, level up our delivery of services more efficiently, and are focused on accountability and a team-focused approach to care.

Stop now and reread that last paragraph. Twice.

Very few clinics do this right. That's just a matter of fact. They are always looking for a marketing scheme or the next big machine or profit center to save them, and they fail to implement consistent processes on things they already have or fail to take advantage of the new things they add. I see it all the damn time. They feel the need to add more and more when they could thrive by just adding consistent effective processes to what they already have in place. It is less expensive to implement efficient and effective processes that add or capture revenue than it is to add a new scheme.

Before we begin, you will find some downloadable assessments in the appendix that you should take to help you assess where you are. Some are simple, yes or no, and others will need some thought. These are for you to see where you are currently in your practice. You need to know where you are to determine where we need to pivot first. Damn you, Ross...... when I wrote that, I thought of Friends and didn't even see that scene till 20 years later. I digress.

Finally, I hope you find this book quick and easy to read. I hope it makes sense and you get some good ideas and strategies you can implement now to start changing your business tomorrow. Some of the processes we teach are simple and inexpensive. For example, everyone I work with starts with a basic sales cycle and the phone auditing/training system. I do this for two reasons: it has the fastest and most significant impact on the business's cash flow, and also because those systems only require a minimal fee so that you do not get hit with a massive bill or a long-term contract. The price for this system costs about what one new paid patient brings in, and the return on investment

(ROI) is immense, so it is a no-brainer. And please send me feedback! I love hearing from everyone else's perspective, and I want to hear about your wins and what else you would like to learn about in other training sessions. After reading this book, if you feel like you might be interested in working with me and my group, email me. 3, 2, 1, off we go.........

Chapter 1

Mistake 1:

Not Having a Detailed Phone Tracking, Recording, and Auditing System.

Implementing this one system can triple your revenue overnight. In all seriousness, you could read this short section, implement the changes, start this system in a couple of hours, and change your practice almost overnight. Applying this process is, BY FAR, the most neglected and the easiest and fastest system to change. Out of all the other things I recommend in this book, whatever you do, please add this system exactly how it is mapped out and do it this week. The following are the steps to get this implemented:

1. Set up a call tracking metrics account online. Call tracking metrics is an online software that measures data and records voice calls. These include call volume, call length,

customer satisfaction, and call center agent performance. Calltrackingmetrics.com helps businesses assess effective marketing strategies and plan advertising budgets. This is super simple and should cost around $40 per month.

2. Once the Call Tracking Metrics account is set up, buy the tracking numbers you need for the different advertising mediums you use, your main website, and Google My Business. The average clinic needs 5 numbers. They cost about $2 per number, so the cost is minimal. It is super simple to do this part. Just click the link below for a 30 second video tutorial.

https://www.loom.com/share/5044b852900c48c1b3074d0612aad528?sid=f9864663-acd5-42fb-90c4-97417e02d49e

3. Train on listening to the calls and have the auditing score sheet out and ready to go. Whoever is responsible for answering the phones should be the first person who audits themselves. Then, you need to go in every week

and audit a few new patients' calls to ensure they accurately hear themselves and score the calls.

4. Set up a bonus system and give the phone receptionist $10 for every new patient who shows up and $3 for anyone showing up for a lecture or sales event.

Below is an explanation of how the phone auditing score sheet works. I will spend some time going through the scoring system to help you understand and train this post. However, I recommend calling me and my team and setting up a time and letting us do the training. Some nuances to this training will take it to the next level. The cost equates to about one new closed cash patient, but this system alone can easily double your practice.

Call Scoring Sheet

You grade performance on each metric on a scale from 1 to 5: 1 = Worst performance possible and 5 = Best performance possible.

Below are the various aspects that you will be graded on. Following that will be an explanation and role-playing for each one. The following is what will be scored and how to assess the score.

1. What is your tone level? _____

2. Was the appointment scheduled? _____

3. Did you use the dual close system to schedule the patient? _____

4. Did you control the conversation? _____

5. Did you answer the patient's questions correctly? _____

6. Did you ask the patients the correct questions? _____

7. Did you show genuine care and concern for the symptoms the patient described? _____

8. Did you get agreements? _____

9. Did you implement negative acknowledgments? _____

10. Did you create a sense of urgency (is the patient scheduled that week)? _____

11. Did you insist that the spouse or S.O. come with the prospective patient and explain the importance of this policy? _____

12. Did you convey that you are there to help, even if it means you have to refer them to another clinic? _____

13. Did you answer questions that should have been deferred to the consult or answered only by the clinician? _____

14. Did you give the patient thorough and accurate directions to the clinic? _____

15. Did you create any objections regarding insurance, money, time, conviction of the plan, distance from the clinic, or attendance of significant other? (-1 through -5) _____

Total points available: 70

Below 60: Weekly training Below 50: Daily training. I know it probably sounds like torture or boot camp but daily training will be necessary until the scores consistently rate above 60. The training is conducted as a three step process. Step 1. We listen to calls together and each score it. Usually the receptionist is very close to the number where I score them. If not- we usually have to take a step back and train on the system again. If you are doing this exercise and you have a staff member who consistently score themselves much higher than you, even when you have been showing her the corrections needed, then you have the wrong person in this post. Step 2. We role play with me being the receptionist and record that call. Then we score that call as well. Step 3. I call as if I am a new patient and we role play the scripts. It usually takes a few weeks to really get the phone receptionist dialed in.

Again, considering we lose so much of our communication (the non-verbal part of human interaction), there is no substitute for a high tone level. The tone of voice in communication is how you use your voice to get your point across. It's how you sound when you say words out loud. The tone of voice conveys your feelings or emotions and can affect how your message is perceived and understood. It's critical for any person providing customer support and service to control how they come across in any conversation. What you say and *how you say it* matters. *Tone* helps to provide added emphasis, intent, and emotion behind your words. Tone can dramatically shift how a conversation proceeds and a message is received, influencing the patient's decision-making If the patient feels like you are listening and caring- you can have a lot of missteps and get the appointment scheduled. However, a low-tone, disengaged phone receptionist will destroy your cash flow faster than anything else.

Let's go through each one.

1. What is your tone level?

The tone of voice is crucial because it influences whether your communication is received positively or negatively. This sets the first impression of the office because a phone call may be the initial contact and, therefore, the first impression of the office. The tone level is simple: does it sound like you are smiling through the phone and upbeat, or do you sound like a drunken pirate on a four-day bender in the middle of an Atlantic gale?

2. Was the appointment scheduled?

One of the most important goals of the new patient call are not creating your objections (there is an entire chapter on this in the Complete Sales Cycle book) and scheduling the appointment. Either they are on the schedule or not.

Believe it or not, because of how our brains work, we typically bring our own buying habits into a scene. It sounds ridiculous, but it's true. We must not say something here that will cause issues for the close with the case manager or physician. We discuss this in more detail in a later chapter. We should not create a thought that gives the patient reasons to object to buying our product or service.

3. Did you use the dual close system to schedule the patient?

The dual-close system is a process of scheduling a patient so that you direct them in making the appointment and by limiting their decision to 2 options for each question. Most people tend to have difficulty making decisions. You can help them decide by providing limited options. This will keep the efficiency of the office while allowing the patient to feel in control. However, you are directing the decision-making/scheduling. You do that by *not* allowing open-ended questions for the patient to answer, such as *"When would you like to come in"* but by giving the patient limited choices. Limiting their options will allow you to control the schedule but make them feel like they are making the decision. This will make scheduling a patient quicker. The way this works is you give the patient limited choices by framing the question to let them pick between two options of your choice. This allows them to feel they are making the decision and speeds up the process. It goes like this.

"Ok, Mr. /Mrs. Awesome, Patient; we can see you this week on Wednesday or Thursday. Which would you prefer?"

They give a response. You then say,

"Awesome. Would you like morning or afternoon?"

After their response, you ask them the final dual question to choose between two-time slots you provide.

"I have 1:00 pm or 3:30 pm. Which time would you prefer."

This drills down when they come in and will decrease the number of reschedules and no-shows.

4. Did you control the conversation?

Controlling a call means being in charge of the direction of the call. It involves getting and conveying information quickly and efficiently so the receptionist can remain productive. This is determined by how long the call lasts. Were you in control of the call, or did you let them ramble on and on and waste 30 min? A solid new patient intake should take no longer than 10 minutes, max.

5. Did you answer the patient's questions correctly?

Patients will have legitimate questions that must be answered correctly. The majority of questions will be the same. By preparing for the most often asked question, we can provide the best answer confidently, quicker and improve compliance. Some examples of frequently asked questions: How long will the appointment take? Is this going to hurt? How much is this going to cost? Is my insurance going to cover this? (this is a MASSIVE objection in the physical medicine and regenerative space but not so much in the Med Spa world)? I hear objections here more than anything else.

6. Did you ask the patient the correct questions?

Asking the correct questions, such as their address and phone numbers, are apparent. However, some probing questions need to be asked. These are very specific questions used to begin the sales cycle, which are discussed in the following chapter. Probing questions also help to AVOID creating objections in the sales cycle. For an overview of intake sheets, look at the appendix at the end of the book for a few examples.

7. Did you show genuine care and concern for the symptoms the patient described?

Did you show genuine concern, or in the case of a med spa, show absolute interest in their situation? For example, if they say they have been told they need surgery, appropriate negative acknowledgments would be, "I hate to hear that," Unfortunately, I hear that all the time, and I am concerned," or "Your symptoms are concerning."

8. Did you get agreements?

Agreements are basic statements when you agree with what the patient is saying. Comments like, "I agree," "I understand," "I know this is frustrating," "I get it," and "I am with you" go a long way. Just stay in agreement as much as possible!

9. Did you implement negative acknowledgments?

Negative acknowledgments show concern and also show you are actively listening. A negative objection is used to build rapport and subconsciously let the patient know this is serious. For example, such statements as, *"That is concerning. We need to get you scheduled this week."* or *"I hate to hear that you are in so much pain."* or *"That does not sound fun at all."* or *"I have heard that same thing from others, and it is not a good sign, let's get you scheduled."*

10. Did you create a sense of urgency?

This is simple. Get the patient scheduled THIS week if you are dealing with a physical medicine patient as fast as possible for any med spa type clients. The statistics are mind-blowing, but if you schedule a patient out more than a week, twenty to thirty percent never show up. Go out two weeks, and it's well over fifty percent. By then, they have already spent their money with your competitor. If you don't believe me, go into your EMR, audit the new patient no-shows, and look at when they called to make their initial appointment. It blows my mind, but I see it more often than not: a new client that is going broke and stressed out allows their staff to schedule new business two to three weeks out because they are too "busy" to see new patients that week (which they never are). With this strategy, you are begging the Universe to put you on your knees and send you to the poor house forever.

11. Did you insist that the spouse or significant other attend the visit with the prospective patient?

One of the most critical pieces of the new patient phone call is asking for the spouse or significant other to come with them to the visit. One of the most common objections from patients at the close is finances. Patients will often need to get an agreement with their spouse or significant other, so you will hear, "I have to go home and talk to my spouse." By having the spouse there, you will get the patient closed, which is most desirable and cuts down on the workload of having to contact the patient or answer questions for the spouse on a different day. The script goes like this:

"Ok, Mr. Patient, we will be going over some important healthcare issues and discussing if you are a good candidate for our care, and you will be making some important decisions about your health. Your healthcare is very important to us. So, do you have a spouse or significant other coming with you? We often find they have some valuable information about your case/condition that can help us with your care. It also allows them to ask questions about your care and have a better understanding. We do not want them to be left out of these decisions".

Most of the time, they will give you their partner's name. Notate the name on the intake sheet so the case manager can acknowledge the significant other when the patient arrives for their appointment. Again, the critical part of this is to allow the case manager the most accessible close of the sale so have the spouse there.

12. Did you answer questions that should have been deferred to the consult or answered only by the clinician?

The script sounds like this:

"Ok, Mrs. Jones. The first thing I want to convey to you is you are important to me. I want to make sure I take care of your needs today. I need to ask you a few questions to see if you might be a good candidate for our care. If you are, we can move forward and get you on the schedule to see the Dr. However, if you are not a good candidate, I will find someone in town who I can refer you to so you can get the help you need. Does that sound fair?"

"Ok, Mrs. Jones. You are important to us, so I want to ensure I handle all your needs today. To do that, I need to ask you a few questions. We want to make sure you are a good candidate for our care. If you are, I'll get you on the schedule to

see the Dr. However, if you are not a good candidate, I will find someone in town who can help you. Does that sound fair?"

When was the last time you heard someone say that on the phone? I never have (except for my clients). This script shows concern, empathy, caring, focus, and attention. It gives a game plan for the call and puts the patient front and center. This script goes further to build rapport than any other thing in the initial call.

14. Did you give the patient thorough and accurate directions to the clinic? _____

When providing directions to the office, keep this simple. You can text them a pin with the address so they can click on it, and it will pop up on their maps. Even old farts can do this now. Unfortunately, people will still get lost and call. I am not joking, I was in one of the clients' practices recently, and I heard the phone receptionist take a call. She was trying to give directions but seemed confused. After a few minutes, the receptionist realized the new patient was sitting IN THEIR PARKING LOT. I swear this is a true story, AND sooner or later, it will happen to you. On the initial call, send them a pin. Keep the call quick and do not waste time with the road-by-road directions unless it is absolutely necessary. Or help them out and email them directions printed off Mapquest.

15. Did you create objections for the patient regarding insurance, money, time, conviction of the plan, distance from the clinic, and attendance of their significant other?

The granddaddy of them all. We find that the staff and provider can create an objection for the patient that the patient didn't even have. This is termed "creating your own objections." An entire book could be written on Objections (I'm confident it already has), and this is one of the most interesting problems I see in the initial call and the consultation. I am not going to spend a lot of time on this here, but typically, we create the objections and hand-deliver them to the new patient, which then becomes an objection for the patient to use. One way to detect these is to start recording calls. You will immediately see what I mean. It is just straight-up bad human psychology, and it never ceases to amaze me that providers and owners swear this phenomenon never happens until they hear firsthand the recordings.

Here are a few examples I have heard, but the list is a mile long:

1. "I live over on that side of town as well. It is such an awful drive in traffic. I hate the commute." This type of negative statement gives the patient a negative reminder of the distance.

2. "Yes, your insurance covers this procedure." especially in a clinic where the procedures are not covered by insurance.

3. "Yes, we will file your insurance for this" or "The services we provide are never covered by insurance." This is a MASSIVE problem for the case manager. When the patient hears this from the phone girl, they come in with the expectation they will not be paying much and are about to get hit with a big bill. It becomes a massive issue for the case manager to overcome during the consult. It's the biggest problem I hear, as crazy as it sounds. It blows my mind when the phone girls create objections.

4. "The cost is around $5000 per procedure. I know, right? That is super expensive. I couldn't afford that!" Crazy as it sounds, I have heard a phone receptionist say these exact words. The correct script for when a potential patient calls and asks how much it will cost is: *"It depends on what the doctor recommends as the best treatment for you. When you come in for the initial consultation, the case manager will review the cost during that visit. That is, of course, if you are a good candidate for our services. Again, our*

biggest concern right now is whether or not we can help you, and like I said earlier, if we can't, we will find out where to send you. Is that fair?"

I deduct points for creating your own objections simply because it is the number one killer of the sale process, and it has to be corrected AT ALL COSTS. Your most significant competitor, by far, is yourself. Focusing on this system and the other five in this book will go a long way to decreasing self-inflicted wounds.

Chapter 2

Mistake Number 2:

Not Understanding the Sales Cycle and the Inability to Convert Expensive Leads, And How to Audit, Role Play, and Close Cash Patients Like a Pro

The Sales Cycle

A sales cycle is a series of steps a practice uses to sell a product or service to a customer. The goal of a sales cycle is to connect with new customers/patients and get them to buy your products and services, and refer their friends and family.

There are generally 7 steps in a sales cycle. These steps include:

1. Prospecting, or lead generation, which is how an organization searches for new patients in their target market

2. Making contact with potential customers

3. Qualifying customers

4. Presenting your offer

5. Overcoming customer objections

6. Closing the sale

7. Generating referrals

You must know and understand the steps in your sales cycle. Each step in the cycle supports the next. A complete understanding can make all the difference in your business's success.

Some of the many benefits to understanding the steps in your sales cycle are; first, you can optimize your team structure to support your sales cycle. For example, if you know your biggest challenge is closing a patient on a service, you can put more team training time into that stage of the sales cycle. Secondly, you can use understanding your sales cycle process to train staff, which makes bringing on and training new staff easy.

You might also notice places where large amounts of effort are being wasted. Knowing your process lets you eliminate low ROI projects and helps your team focus on the actions that give you the most results. Finally, you can better pinpoint which steps in the sales cycle need improvement. You might discover that your team is excellent at generating leads but needs to improve at making contact. Because you can pinpoint this, you can now focus training on how to improve.

I realize some of you cringe thinking about having to sell something or being in sales. Sales have an unfairly bad reputation. Salespeople are perceived to be pushy, sneaky, and annoying, so many people want to avoid being associated with sales. However, in Grant Cardone's book "Sell or Be Sold," he brings up a critical piece of information. In all human communication, we are either selling or being sold, even with our kids. Trying to get them to get out the door faster or when they try to convince you they NEED the candy bar at the store, you are in the midst of a sales cycle. Understanding the sales cycle can also effectively be applied to other aspects of life.

We will go through the steps of the sales cycle one by one. There isn't a business out there that can't benefit from learning, understanding, and implementing sales cycles.

When does the sales cycle begin?

A. When they walk in the front door

B. see your marketing

C. make the first call, in the room for the consult

? All of these are important, but the answer is with your marketing. The message and content you convey with your marketing are critical for your success in closing a patient care plan. Marketing needs to be strategically crafted, placed, and properly worked to prepare the leads for the sales cycle. We have websites, Facebook ads, lectures, and, most importantly, a strategic partner with a solid, effective system for new and old patients. We have been doing this for over 15 years with very repeatable statistics. So if you need someone to help you with marketing, please email me for details. drben@regenmedicalconsulting.com

The next critical step in the sales cycle after marketing is handling the phones. Every clinic I have worked with has been unable to get a grip on how their phones are answered. Most need help understanding how and why this can make or break their practice. I have an entire book on the phones, including how to audit and score the calls. It may be hard to believe, but correctly handling your phones can double your practice practically overnight with NO extra advertising spending or increase in overhead. I have audited thousands of calls over the years, and I can't stress enough that in the first phone call, your staff can create objections that will impact your financial close. When I was in practice, I heard that repeatedly but resisted believing it until I finally took a closer look at what was being said and saw the seeds of objection planted in the patients' minds. Waiting as long as I did to address this issue was very costly.

All clinics should have checklists for their processes in the office. These checklists make sure the steps are completed in order and not missed. Lists can also help reduce errors and mistakes in the process. As part of the sales cycle, a new patient checklist should cover each action, starting with the first call and working through the patient walking in the door.

This list should include:

> 1. Was the call audited and scored, paying attention to any potential objections being created?

2. Was the patient called and reminded several times about the appointment?

3. Was a text message reminder sent?

4. Was a text sent with a location pin for the office?

5. Was a video sent that shows how to get to the office?

Once the patient walks in the door, the patient's routing checklist is as follows:

1. Was the patient greeted with intention?

2. Was the patient offered coffee or water?

3. Was the patient given clean copies of the paperwork?

4. Was the patient seated in a clean, comfortable chair?

5. Was the patient's spouse or significant other greeted, acknowledged, and validated?

Before you even get to the checklist, it is an essential piece of this puzzle to have a clear understanding of the reasons why a patient would want the services you offer, why they need you to be their provider, and why they should choose your company as opposed to the guy down the street who is charging 20% less. This needs to be comprehended by you and conveyed clearly to your staff. You can't successfully sell something you don't believe in, and every person working in your office is part of that sales cycle. You should feel confident that you are comfortable with each of those questions before you attempt to sell your goods and services.

Exercise:

I would like you to take a moment to list these reasons here.

Why THESE Services?

_____

_____

_____

_____

_____

Why YOU as a provider?

_____

_____

_____

_____

Why should YOUR company provide the services?

_____

_____

_____

_____

Now that you have completed this step, let's continue with some thought and idea-generating exercises. I want to build a foundation for your success. These exercises will help ensure you have the pieces to 10X your sales process and income. You must establish and build confidence in why these patients should have faith in you, your services, and your practice. These must be shared with your staff, and they must buy-in. Then everyone should work through the rules of the sales cycle. Sales cycles need to be completely ethical and use the following guidelines:

1. Keep them super simple.

2. They need to be transparent.

3. Make your intentions known.

4. Qualify them with hard questions.

5. Be focused on getting agreements from the buyer.

6. Show a financial proposal to every patient.

7. Use a third party if needed.

8. Frame the second sale.

9. Show concern for any potential health problems with the patient's significant other.

10. Have a system in place for massive follow-up.

Exercise:

What sales opportunities are you currently using from this list? (circle)

Which ones should you be using that you are not? (check mark)

Incoming calls

Sold customers (second sale)

Referrals

Unsold patients

Website

Complaints

Email campaigns

Social media posts

The next thing you need to do is track the stats of your sales cycle. Any stat you track and follow, you are more likely to change. Let's write down some of the stats we need to track regarding the sales cycle. By the way, I will have a comprehensive stat write-up in the Systems volume released in September 2023.

I will list a few now, but please write down any others you think you would like to track in the box below.

  1. Amount of money spent on marketing (ad budget, PER vertical)

  2. Number of responses, including any phone calls and text messages/ Facebook IMs (we will

deal with answering the phones and follow up later)

3. Appointments scheduled

4. New patient appointments

5. No shows

6. Consult time in minutes

7. Number of consults closed

8. Amount of dollars in revenue total per close

9. ROI on the ad spend of each profit vertical.

10. Amount of money spent on bonuses per vertical.

Can you think of anything else? Write them below.

_____

_____

_____

When you have established and built confidence in why these patients should have faith in you, your services, and your practice, you should share that with your staff. It would help if you worked through the sales cycle steps with the team.

Let's dive into the nuts and bolts of the actual Financial Consultation or, as some call it, the Report of Findings/Recommendations. This is the nuts and bolts of a consultation. You can tinker with this system to suit the particular profit vertical you are working at the moment. However, the overall design should always be linear, with the result being an acknowledgment that the patient understands everything laid out in front of them, and they have decided to either 1. Start the therapy/treatments, or 2. You immediately put them into the follow-up system.

Any italicized sentences below are possible role-play and practice scripts, so please take note..

The Sales Cycle Soup to Nuts.

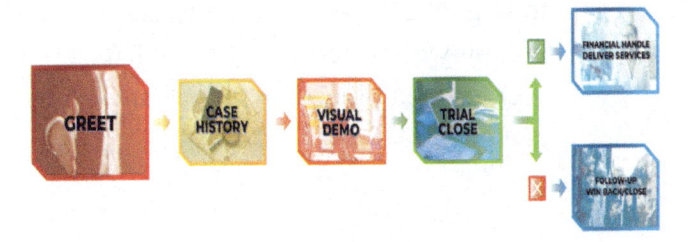

STEP 1: PREPARE

You want to clear your head before you walk into the room. The most critical steps for you to think about and remind yourself before you start it to remember the first impression is vital. Make it count.

1. Remember that the close is for them, not you. They are there to get life-changing help, and this 30-minute window is about THEM, not you. You get paid to find out what they need- and give it to them. They need to *feel* like you are giving them what they NEED.

2. Be super mindful to LISTEN for any objections. The true masters of the sales cycle know this and are hypervigilant at listening for and addressing

any objections immediately before they continue through the cycle (we will discuss this later). You will only close people once you have handled ALL of their objections, which are simply complaints.

3. Remember how you buy for yourself. Be mindful of the type of person you are talking to. What personality type are they? Each person is a unique combination of four personality types. Many books are written on how to communicate and sell to each kind, so the point is to be mindful. For example, an analytical personality will often be an accountant or engineer. These individuals need detailed information, numbers, and statistics and prioritize logic. Knowing that helps you in presenting your report of findings.

4. You create your own objections (more on that later) based on your own buying habits, so keep it at the top of your mind to listen for YOUR buying objections and habits as well. Trust me, we all

STEP 2: THE GREETING

This is more like a handoff from either the front desk or the case manager. It would help if someone introduced you, and they need to say something nice and affirmative to the prospective client when they introduce you.

Example: *Ok, Mrs. Butler, this is Nicole, and she is our expert on body contouring (Decompression, Neuropathy, Regen Medicine, Facelifts, etc. etc. whatever, and she is always ready and happy to get to understand your particular needs and help you (insert lost weight, look younger, feel better, get out of pain- whatever is appropriate here).*

Then you smile, shake their hand and tell them your name and that you are excited to meet and help them. Handle the presence or non-presence of the spouse or decision-maker. Every patient who walks in the door should have their spouse or decision-maker with them if they are there for any medical treatments (anything other than body contouring and laser facelifts).

Script 1.

Thank you for coming in this morning. I intend to ensure I understand your needs correctly and you know your options. I will also show you all the benefits of our care plans in the practice so you get the best results possible. Does that sound fair to you? GET THE AGREEMENT. *Great!*

It is also my goal, if you qualify for our plan, to get you started on the plan today and get you on the road to health (out of pain, looking younger, losing weight...you fill in the blank depending on the treatment).

Before we begin- I want to ask a very important question. On a scale from one to ten, with ten being the most important and 1 being the least, where are you in your mind in regards to how serious you are about getting this handled today?

IF you hear a number 7 or less.

STOP immediately! Ask the question again. *So you said a 5. Are you sure that is where you are today? I just want to make sure I understand because you mentioned in your paperwork this is a serious issue.*

See if you can work your way to get them up to an 8 or higher with this script.

Say- *Ok. I appreciate the honesty. Thank you.*

To be entirely upfront and honest with you, we only move forward with these consults when a patient is highly motivated to get the help they need. You have to be a willing participant in your health care, and what we have found after (however long you have been in practice- or say thousands of patients) that anyone not engaged and all in on their program will not get the results they are looking for because they are not as serious about the program as they should be. Does that make sense? Good.

We cannot care more about your healthcare and results than you do.

This particular scene will only happen sometimes. It rarely occurs with the proper advertising, but you will see it on some Groupon and Facebook ads when you offer a free demo or service. You will always attract a small percentage of tire kickers just looking for a procedure for free. If you are new, I understand this kind of marketing to get people in the door as a loss leader, but eventually, that kind of offer will do absolutely nothing in a positive manner for the practice.

PRACTICE THESE SCRIPTS!

Answer these questions for the *Greeting* portion of the Sales Consultation based on a scale of 1-5.

1. Did you greet the patient and introduce yourself by your name? 1-5

2. Acknowledge the spouse 1-5

3. Identify who is in charge 1-5

4. Follow the spouse thank you script 1-5

5. Put the patient at ease 1-5

6. Kept a positive tone level 1-5

STEP 3: FACT FINDING

As mentioned earlier, probing questions help obtain information used as an essential part of the sales cycle. You must discover the patient's dominant buying motive. This requires you to dig deep into your fact-finding when your consultations are in process. This can be challenging, but finding your patient's dominant buying motive can make or break your sale. For example, if the patient is in your office for hormone therapy, you must find their motivating factor. Are they there because they want to lose weight, for better sexual performance, brain fog, or a lack of energy?

You can also use this opportunity to create more awareness to their problem. This will strengthen their motivation. For example, ask the patient where they will see themselves in the next fifteen years if they do not fix their problems. And whether their problem has worsened or improved in the last one to five years. Get a clear understanding of what they have tried before that hasn't worked. Then use this opportunity to explain how your treatment stands apart from what they have already tried. You can better close a sale if you know what your patient wants, you increase their awareness of the problem and you help them see that what they have been doing to address the problem is not working. If the spouse is in charge and keeps interrupting, be mindful that he/she is the one you are actually closing. They aren't going to agree to spend thousands of dollars for something they don't feel their partner needs.

It helps to grade the fact-finding from your recorded consults.

Did you ask the right questions? 1-5

Did you get a real answer? 1-5

Did you ask bad questions? 1-5

Did you ask at least three probing questions to get the real answer? 1-5

Did you find their dominant buying motive? 1-5

Did you discover how they make their decisions? 1-5

I recommend that any scores on the questions above between 15 and 22 require daily role-play. 22-30 points role play weekly. Anything below 15 points should require a personality test to determine if they are appropriately assigned to this position and should role-play daily.

Look at your score above and ask yourself: did YOU create an objection? DEDUCT 1-5 points. Then run a lap around the block and do 100 push-ups for penance. This is, BY FAR, the most mind-blowing thing I hear when auditing phone calls and consults, and it is an absolute killer in the sales cycle.

Let me give you a couple of examples that I hear frequently.

Phone receptionist: *"What is your address?"*

Patient responds.

Receptionist: "*Oh! I live over there on that side of town as well. The traffic has gotten SO bad! I hate the commute.*"

In this instance, the receptionist has created an objection for the patient to close. I have also seen this:

The Case Manager or Dr. will say, "*I see you live over in West Jefferson. Me too! I love it over there, but I hate the traffic.*"

Here are another couple of objections that make me blow my lid in frustration:

When the case manager gets to the financial close, they say something along these lines: "*I know it sounds like a lot of money but....*" or how about, "*I agree coming to 12 visits is going to be a lot of time, money and gas.*"

You must pay close attention to creating what I term "your own objections." Creating your own objections creates problems with the close, which is why the system penalizes you for this act of madness.

Each office type is different in how they need to craft questions and avoid creating your own objections. We have created a few templates available to help implement this system so you can make it specific to your needs. Just email me at drben@regenmedicalconsulting.com

STEP 4: DEMO

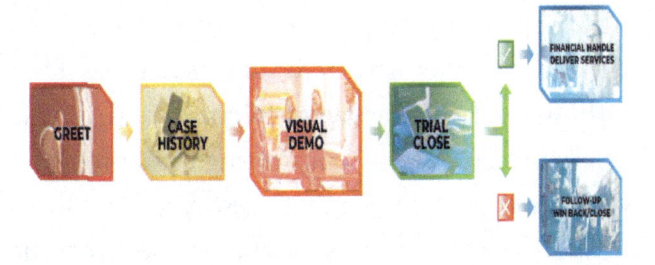

Demo Scoring System

1. Did you talk too much about your product or use any big technical words?

2. Did you relate your procedure to THEIR specific needs?

3. Did you show them AT LEAST one visual and one testimonial? Remember, a picture is worth 1000 words.

4. Did you get an agreement from the patient? For example, in the aesthetics/body contouring/weight loss space, you should literally hear something like the word WOW come out of their mouths. If you are doing something like neuropathy, have them POINT out the picture (X-ray of a knee, MRI of a disc lesion, thermal image of their feet in a neuropathy case...). Aesthetic

practices should rely on before and after photos to show improvements previous patients have gotten in the same areas being treated for this patient. There is nothing like before and after pictures regarding laser facials, botox, or body contouring. As a pre-frame, our website design has several of these as a slider so the prospective patient can slide the mouse across the face to the before and after, which is an excellent effect. Go to Aiken Anti-Aging to see the effect. It is powerful and can be done for any vertical you promote in your office. We also highly recommend using a ton of video testimonials on your website to help social proof your clinic. Websites are dead now, and people do not really go there for anything other than basic research and social proofing.

5. Also, human beings are all very visually stimulated. Having an MRI or X-ray of affected areas in decompression, chiropractic, or practices that deal with joint pain gives you a way to point out exactly where their issues lie and how to address them. Aesthetic practices should rely on before and after photos to show improvements previous patients have seen in the areas being treated.

6. DO NOT try to close a patient on care until they give you an agreement that they SEE and FEEL where

they are right now and where they will be after your plan.

They need to distinguish and understand where they are and where they are heading with your plan.

7. Did you handle all their objections up to this point?? Script: *Is there anything you have seen thus far that would stop you from starting the care plan now?* This step is CRITICAL for several reasons. First, you will almost always hear the biggest objection right here. Actively listen to what they say and be ready for a response. At this point, the only real objection you should hear is a money or time/stall objection.

If the spouse or decision maker is not present, you should be prepared to hear, *"I have to talk to my spouse."* We will handle that specific objection and many more in the next chapter.

NEVER FORGET THIS- This concept is so important! *WORDS* are the most misunderstood aspect of a sales cycle. The patient wants to *FEEL* and have positive *EMOTIONS* that you can take them from where they are to the final result they are looking for no matter what the procedure is you are providing.

STEP 5: TRIAL CLOSE

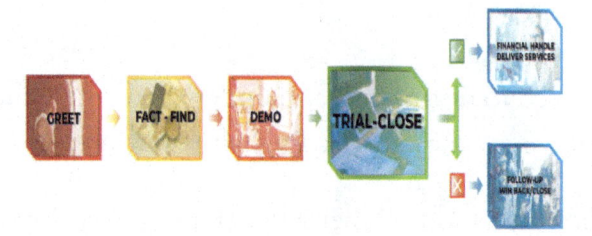

The questions you need to ask and be obvious with before moving the patient to the close are:

1. Have you seen enough to make a decision about starting up with care?

2. Do you need to see any more information, or do you feel like you are ready to get started?

If the answer to either of these questions is no, you have missed something in the fact-finding, the demo, or you created an objection somewhere in the process. The only way to combat this is to start the sales cycle over. The master at closing always knows where they are in the sales cycle and with the objections. This is why the Case Manager needs to understand and be trained on what objections they are likely to encounter and how to handle them properly, and know how to use the hard questions.

You cannot be afraid to get nosy and ask questions that may be a little uncomfortable but are necessary to get critical information to guide the patient to make their own conclusion that they are in need of your services. Some examples are:

What are you going to do if your spouse says no?

Where are you going to go if your PCP says no?

Have his/her recommendations worked for you so far?

Would you agree the only thing the surgeon is going to do is surgery, which is dangerous?

They have the same laser we have.

NEVER let yourself get into a position where the patient says they are going to shop around. You also want to be unaware if the patient has already been to another clinic and wanted to see what you had to offer. If this happens, it means that most of the filters (systems) we use to avoid this scene have been ignored, and you are in a real bind here.

Your only way to salvage this is to offer massive value. NEVER drop your price, just add massive value. These cash services are lucrative, so offer one free session on body contouring or a free laser treatment on the face.

The CLOSE Scoring system.

1. Did you ask the correct questions and get to the dominant buying motive from the patient?

2. Did you negotiate pricing or remain firm?

3. Did you create your own objections?

4. Did you set the frame for the close correctly?

5. Did you ask the hard questions? Example: "*What are you going to do if they say no?*"

6. Did you present the financials with the correct tone?

7. Did you shoot for the trial close with one of the two questions?

8. Did you handle their objections and find the unspoken one if it was presented?

9. Did you control the conversation?

10. Did you put the patient into the follow-up system if they didn't close and send them a thank you text within 30 minutes of them leaving the office?

Bonus 1:

The Easiest Referral System Ever

Here is one of the easiest and fastest ways to increase revenue without spending a dime on advertising. Most internet marketers would call this the upsell or second sale. I have heard numerous versions of this system ranging from a once-a-month "Referral Day" to a door prizes giveaway like a free TV or toaster. Weight loss clinics may have a Cutco knife system laid out upfront. Some clinics even put the TV at the check-in station and have lovely colorful balloons tied to the TV. Seen it a million times. This sounds great but there can be regulatory issues involving kickback and enticement that can get you into some serious trouble. For that reason I would not recommend these types of marketing efforts. If you do decide to do them, make sure you check with a healthcare attorney to assure you are not violating any regulations.

1. In an effort to keep this short, the easiest way to get a referral is to just ask. Yes, just ASK, but

you must do it in the correct manner to get the best result. So just keep it simple and use the system outlined below.
2. The system itself is easy, and it goes like this. You train your staff to listen and ask a couple of questions every time a patient comes into the office (see below). Anytime a patient gives you an agreement or says anything positive about your office, staff, or the results, you have someone ask for a referral. And it would sound/look something like this.
    a. The front staff gives the patient some kind of compliment, such as,

    "I love your purse."

    "I love your sweater."

    "Awesome shoes"

This is to get the patient into an agreement and an acknowledgment. People love like-minded and complementary staff.

    b. The treating MD, DO, PA, DC, PT, Aesthetician, or whoever is working with the patient will then ask,

"So, how are we doing? What can we do better? I would love your input so we can improve."

Ask if they are enjoying their visits and getting results. If they say no, listen for and address any objection! You want patients to have a positive experience at your office. If they say anything positive about the staff or their results, then that staff member will use this script:

"That is so great to hear. We love to hear that we are doing a good job (getting massive results). I am curious, do you have any friends or family you can think of that have the same issue that we could reach out to and see if we can help them get (insert whatever the results are for the vertical you are working in)?"

Most of the time, they will say no, which is ok. Just add in something like,

"Ok, I understand. Do you have any neighbors or coworkers?"

At this point, one of two things will happen. Either they will think of someone after you have opened their options of people to think about, or they will say no.

In the case of the no, say,

"That's *ok. We love helping people, and if you can think of anyone later, just let me know at your next visit."*

Don't worry, 9 times out of 10 they will come to their next visit and have someone in mind.

If they say yes, ask them for the potential patient's name. Put the patient's name on the back of a business card and circle your number. Then write the referral's name in the chart for the next visit. On the next visit, ask the patient how the referral is doing and ask,

"Do you think you could connect me to (referral's name) on a text thread?"

This part is tricky, but you should be able to read the room with your patient and know if this last part would work. At a minimum, after you ask how they are doing, you should ask the patient if they had a chance to talk to them about your clinic (most of the time, they will say no).

The whole point of this is to get the staff used to asking for referrals (asking the universe for abundance) and then using a system of getting names to follow up with and having your current patient list help you market your services. If they are body contouring/weight loss or aesthetics patients this system is even easier. You could dumb it all the way down to just showing them their progress pictures and then asking, *"has anyone else noticed how much weight you have lost/ how much younger you look?"* Once they say a name, simply ask, "Do you *think she would like to love 30 pounds as well (or look 10 years younger, etc.)?"*

Just remember with this system it is free. It is easy. Track the names, and make it a stat. Just that simple.

Bonus 2:

Handling Objections

This section is about the most important of the entire guide and where most of the role-play happens, so whatever you do, reference this section with all new patients and make sure you role-play these scripts.

We have discussed how the sales cycle looks, but let me add it here one more time to remind you of how it looks:

GREET → CASE HISTORY → VISUAL DEMO → TRIAL CLOSE → ✓ → FINANCIAL HANDLE DELIVER SERVICES
                                                    ✗ → FOLLOW-UP WIN BACK/CLOSE

There are significant reasons why you and your staff need to focus on this particular system during. You might get an objection anywhere in the sales cycle, so you must be prepared to handle them. This is what destroys a sales cycle. If you do not handle all the objections, you will not get a close. If objections are appropriately handled as they occur, it sets everything up for easy and successful closing. This is very important and should be trained and role-played weekly.

Read that again.

So far in this book, we have gone over the correct mindset, the basics of the sales cycles, and a few examples of the scripts we will use to help keep you in control of the consultation. After this section, you will have a much better understanding of the nuances of the sales cycle with some specific scripts. You will also have a much better grip on scoring the consultation because you can pick up on objections. I will even give you a few real-world examples that have been transcribed off the phone system of a real-world clinic.

Reviewing transcripts for phone conversations is the most exciting part of my training with the clinics I consult. Once I teach this section and spend some time role-playing, the results are dramatic, and the cash flow starts to change quickly. Let's dig into the rules of the objections, and then we can work through how we will handle them inside the sales cycle frame.

- Rule number 1: Objections are just complaints. Remember this when you hear one in the sales cycle. Being ready for them makes them much less stressful, and understanding you have just heard one when communicating with the patient will dramatically decrease their power.
- Rule number 2: The more you hear them and role-play for the most common three or four you always hear, the easier it becomes to overcome them, and your close rates will increase very quickly!
- Rule number 3: Once you are trained to hear one, ALWAYS stop and handle the objection immediately. You must isolate the objection and handle it one at a time. Never move past it without a handle, and once you think it has been handled, ask a question like, "Are there any other concerns?" "Did I answer that question for you?" or "Do you feel like you have a better understanding now?" to ensure you and the patient are on the same page.
- Rule number 4. You create your own objections. It's crazy and hard to believe, but you do. I did it myself until I learned how to avoid it.

There are only 5 types of objections and, luckily for you, in the medical space, we usually only have to deal with three of them. Here are the 5 objections:

1. **Time**: It will take too long, or they can't commit to numerous visits.

2. **Stall**: Rarely an issue in healthcare.

3. **Source objection**: A prospect may be okay with the product, procedure, or the program you use to treat their issue but have uncertainties about doing business with the salesperson or company (include yourself here, as they may not like your staff or you. However, this is not a reason to stop them from buying).

4. **Money**: By far the most common objection in healthcare.

5. **The unspoken one:** This is a legitimate problem since you do not know what is preventing them from moving forward. There are numerous examples of this, and these patients usually end up in the follow-up sequence until they are ready to move forward with your program.

What are the 4 biggest objections you consistently hear on a daily basis? Write them below.

_____

_____

_____

_____

By far, the two most significant objections you will get are money or that they think your program will not work for them. It may end up being both. Now let's go over how to address these objections and map out specific handles.

1.   When you get an objection thrown your way, immediately acknowledge it and get an agreement. Just say something along these lines of, *"I get it," "I understand," or "Thanks for sharing."*

2. Isolate it with phrases like, *'Is there anything else you want to tell me?" "Is there anything else stopping you from starting our program besides money?" "If I can solve this one issue, would anything else stop you from starting our care today?"* This is a good one to use when you are down to just money being an issue.

3. If you are having an issue finding the real objection and are still not closing, use a phrase like this: *"We seem to be at a stall here, and I just want to ask you, what is the real concern? Do you think this program will not work for you?"*

Once you are at the end of handling an objection, even if you have to handle more, say, *"You mentioned earlier you must do something to handle your problem, and I agree. I was wondering what will you do if you don't do our_____(Insert your procedure or program)?"* This puts you in a position of strength because they have to give you an answer. Remember, you are there to help them get through the buying process, and the close is for THEM, not YOU. You are there to help them get what they need! Please do not feel bad for asking tough questions, as that is the only way to help them help themselves.

Bonus 3:

Role Play

Role play is a must-have in any practice and is critical to having successful phone calls and consults.

I like to climb big mountains.

Two of the biggest I've climbed are Mount Kilimanjaro and Elbrus. My experiences were completely different with the two despite them being the same height and having identical weather conditions. Before Kilimanjaro, I had spent two weeks in the hospital and was not caring for my body how I should have. I was struggling fifteen minutes into the climb and had to take Dexamethasone every day to handle the pain in my body, which on the first day was the worst I had ever experienced. When I climbed Elbrus, I was healthy and thirty pounds lighter. It was a piece of cake comparatively. I felt like I could have done it twice. I mention this because it is an excellent example of what a vast difference comes with proper training, preparation, and attention. I set myself up for success. To run a successful practice, you must do the same and set yourself up for success. No sports team shows up to a game without having practiced, not even the Bad News Bears.

This is where role play comes in. Consider it practice for the game. It must be on your schedule for all staff every single week. If you have a case manager and would like them to join our weekly training sessions, email me at drben@regenmedicalconsulting.com to have them added to my Zoom training.

In the office, you need to have these role-play sessions for phones, greeting, and handoffs for your consultations and to your case manager—everyone in the office should role-play on handling objections. I send my clients detailed scripts and expect them to be followed at all times by all staff. You want everyone to practice these scripts with other staff and grade them as a pass/fail until they get a firm pass. Make it light and fun. Gamify it if you'd like. You don't want anyone to dread it, or it will eventually get dropped.

Here is the basic overview of the role-play system:

Every organized team in the country practices before games. Some sports, like football, have full pre-seasons, and others, like Baseball, have Spring Training. It is a time for the cream to rise to the top, and the coaches can figure out who and what they have talent-wise on a roster. Even Pee Wee baseball teams practice, and all the players are terrible.

It blows my mind that almost none of the teams I have ever worked with practice or partake in role-play as a means to improve the patient experience. This would help them get better at closing patients on the care. Patients will get care from somewhere, whether it is with you or someone else. I have only worked with three offices that made role-play and practice a consistent habit, and mine was one of them, before I became their consultant. 95 percent of everyone out there avoids this process.

Why? Frankly, they either 1. Think they are too good and should not have to practice. 2. They are just straight-up lazy, or 3. They have just never been taught the value of this process and learned how to do it properly.

Here is a rundown of all the places in the patient experience where you can and should practice:

1. Greeting the patient at the front desk.
2. Delivering their paperwork and offering water.
3. Handing them off to the Case Manager.

4. All four phases of the consult.
5. The financial close. This is a must! PLEASE practice this one.
6. The handoff to the staff that A. Will begin treatments or B. Will start the follow-up sequence on the clients who did not close.
7. Taking the family picture with all the staff and the new patient.

I left out the phone call role play because that is its entire system and needs to be handled with a whole program specific to the phones. However, practicing and role-playing the phones is CRITICAL for practice success. In all those instances above, remember that you should treat the new patients exactly how you want to be treated.

We mention role-playing a lot, so we should discuss the importance and how it is done. Role-playing is a powerful training tool often used in various fields, from business to healthcare to education. It allows individuals to simulate real-life situations, explore different perspectives, and practice problem-solving in a safe and controlled environment. Here's how to incorporate role-playing into your training programs:

1. Identify the Learning Objective: Determine the key learning outcomes from the role-play exercise. This might include improving communication skills, enhancing empathy, handling difficult situations and objections, or practicing specific technical skills.

2. Design the Scenario: Create realistic situations that align with your learning objectives. This scenario should mimic real-life situations that the participants may encounter in their roles. For instance, front desk training may include how to answer specific questions that a patient may have so that it helps with closing the sales cycle, or office manager training, a scenario that might involve handling an angry customer.

3. Assign Roles: Assign roles to each participant. These roles should be clearly defined and relevant to the scenario. Make sure each participant understands their role and what's expected of them.

4. Conduct the Role-Play: Begin the role-playing exercise. Have staff simulate the scenario and have a facilitator or trainer present to guide the activity.

6. Debrief: After the role-play, discuss what happened. This is an opportunity for participants to reflect on their performance, give and receive feedback, discuss

what they learned, and make corrective actions and train

7. Repeat: Role-play exercises are most effective when done repeatedly, allowing participants to practice their skills and apply the feedback they've received.

Role-playing is essential in effective training for several reasons: It allows participants to practice skills safely before applying them in real-life scenarios. This hands-on experience will reinforce learning and increase confidence. Role-playing can help participants understand other perspectives, increasing empathy and improving interpersonal skills while assisting participants to develop their problem-solving and decision-making skills. By confronting simulated challenges, they can experiment with different strategies and learn from their mistakes without real-world consequences. Role-playing provides immediate feedback and reflection opportunities, which are crucial for learning and improvement. Participants can learn from their own experiences and from observing others. Role-playing is a versatile and effective training tool. It provides practical experience, promotes perspective-taking, enhances problem-solving skills, enables feedback and reflection, and boosts engagement, making it an essential addition to your training program.

The following list the basics for conducting role-play training in practices I work with. I will focus on the consult part and offer a couple of examples. Just make sure to keep it light and remind the staff that this is not an exercise to get them in trouble and they can't do anything wrong. Never criticize them in this exercise, and make fun of yourself as much as possible. New staff will be a little shy about it, and it is imperative to make sure this is not an exercise that is on the calendar to be dreaded or a means of punishment for bad stats.

1. Decide which script you will be using.
2. Decide who is going to be doing the role-play exercise.
3. Make sure the two people are facing each other and not too far apart (remember that all human communication is between two people only, so do not try this with three or more at a time).
4. Pick who goes first.
5. Read the script word for word.
6. The receiving partner will say either pass or fail. You pass when you have communicated the script correctly and with some authority and

conviction. You fail if you change the words or do not show complete competence in the script.
7. Switch the roles and do it again.
8. Repeat till a pass is given.

Here are a few simple tips:

- At the beginning, use the written script to help memorize it (gradient training).

- Do not stress out about not making constant eye contact. That is a bit weird and off-putting.

- Do not change the script, and don't sweat screwing up. This is why we are practicing.

Chapter 3

Mistake Number 3.

Not Having a Detailed Marketing Plan And How it is Costing You Millions

Here we will discuss one of the most important systems you will implement in your organization. You will learn that, despite your credentials as a medical professional, when asked what you do for a living, your answer should always be "marketing," not "doctoring." We will be breaking down this chapter into several sections that will clear up several misconceptions right now.

Most medical consultants I know go through a basic evaluation of a clinic and map out the good, the bad, and the ugly. They seem to be offering solutions to the problems, usually by recommending the standard guidance: which employees should be replaced, what profit verticals should be added, which equipment should be purchased to get the tax write-off, and whether to downsize or expand. However, the strategy they encourage the most is to focus immediately on marketing.

Market more. Allocate more of your money to marketing. Find creative ways to attract new patients to enter the door…with marketing. New patients mean more revenue and fewer problems.

The problem is that this strategy doesn't always pay off in the real world. I have seen two clinics close their doors because of this exact strategy. These examples were both in a difficult place and, while I hate to make assumptions, probably would have closed their doors sooner or later. Desperate to salvage their businesses, they spent $10,000 to buy into a system that provided little to no return, lost the last of their financial resources, and were forced to throw in the towel.

 These unfortunate circumstances likely could have been avoided had they first put their focus and intention on building their foundation via a solid set of standard operations. Had they taken this step, they could have avoided losing their livelihood. Not implementing structured operations before initiating marketing will ensure you create several problems you will have a difficult time overcoming down the road. Later in the book, we will review these operations and processes, including phones, scripting, sales cycles, role play, auditing consults, handling follow-up, and managing patient objections. My clients and their staff are rigorously trained on all these dynamics every week, which has been critical to their success.

Let me be clear: I absolutely want you to market the hell out of your clinic. I want you EVERYWHERE. I want you marketing so much that the people in your community complain they are tired of your face. They see your face and hear your name in their sleep and have no choice but to schedule an appointment. Grant Cardone hits the nail on the head when he says, "Obscurity is always your biggest problem."

So what is marketing and advertising? Marketing is all of the company's activities to get its product or service into the marketplace, and advertising is a tactic used to execute that strategy. Advertising is the practice of creating and distributing messages to promote a product, service, or idea. Marketing is the overall process of driving in business.

A successful clinic requires effective marketing strategies to attract a large volume of business. The purpose of marketing is to attract more business than the clinic can handle. To achieve this, focusing on reach and frequency is crucial, targeting specific audiences and ensuring that they hear your message frequently.

When it comes to marketing, it is simple; people have to know who you are, where you are, and what you do. Then you want to create a strong brand image. This can be done through various mediums, such as commercials, billboards, internet and social media ads, print media, and community outreach programs. By generating interest in potential patients, you can attract more business and see great results. However, it is vital to remember that careless marketing can limit profits.

To market your clinic effectively, you must identify and reach your target markets frequently with a clear message. Your target audience should know who you are, what services you offer, and what sets you apart from your competitors. This requires professionalism in all aspects of your marketing materials, from first contact to last. Remember, everything you do is a reflection of your organization and should be something you take pride in.

 I am going to stop right here for a moment to stress that if you do not have any interest in consistent scheduled training on operations and procedures and if you have no desire to focus on marketing or think you are too good at what you do to market, or don't buy into these points, feel free to email me right now. I will refund you the cost of the book. These are the foundational principles in the processes I recommend, and attempting to build the remaining blocks without this foundation will cause your entire structure to crumble.

When your operations and procedures are in place, and you are ready to start ramping up the marketing. The order in which you should focus your attention is as follows:

1. Yourself
2. Your staff
3. New patients
4. Money

Yourself
Marketing yourself may seem strange, but it's essential. By focusing on your commitment to serving your community, your belief in your ability to heal and save lives, and your dedication to your work, you'll attract new patients who will appreciate your love and compassion. Remember that in the Art section, we emphasize the Law of Karma- you get back what you give. Many books have been written about this principle, and it can be a powerful tool for success.

Your Staff
Your staff is critical when it comes to building a cultural climate that promotes success. You have to hire

people who believe in you, believe in what you do, and support and understand your mission and values. Without this buy-in from the men and women who perform most of the day-to-day tasks that keep a clinic going, you will never have a cohesive team that will invest in backing the growth of your business.

New Patients
Attracting new patients is crucial for any practice, especially a new one. However, it's essential to remember that this is a long-term game. Rather than hunting for new patients, think of yourself as a farmer planting seeds. The investments you make today can pay off in the future. Every interaction with a patient, every speaking engagement or program you host, and every marketing effort you undertake has the potential to attract new patients. Even if they don't need your services right now, they may in the future. By planting these seeds today, you increase the likelihood that they'll call you when the time comes.

Case in point: I unexpectedly had two people call my new cell phone number that had never been tied to any of my practices. Both were referred by old patients and had somehow seen a four-year-old newspaper ad. I have no idea how they tracked me down, but I was able to refer them to another practice to receive care. Seeds planted half a decade ago grew into two new opportunities for those patients and the clinic where they were seen.

Naturally, the number of potential new patients you have come through the door determines your number of consult and sales cycle opportunities. When looking at your overhead and the cash flow you need to keep your doors open, you need to break it down to the value of each patient that signs up for care. You must factor in how many referrals you could receive from each new patient. Referrals equate to free advertising (we will go through a system that will show you how to get referrals from the local doctors later - it is a new piece to the marketing puzzle that is incredibly exciting to dig into.) Once you have figured out the referrals you are receiving from current patients, you can project the number of closes you need per month and set a goal to meet that number WEEKLY. We want you to be operating in severe abundance, not desperate and rubbing two nickels together to pay the electric bill.

Money
Whoever spends the most money and effort to acquire a new patient wins. Period. One of my mentors, Grant

Cardone, drives this home in his book, If You're Not First, You're Last. The book goes into detail as to how being first is the only position to be in. If you are in a big enough market, second is acceptable; however, you must believe yourself worthy of being in first position at all times in any market. You have to believe in what you do, your team, and your ability to provide a standard of care far above what your competitors offer. By dominating your marketing and investing in the patients you have yet to bring in the door, you will manifest the volume and quality of patients you need and desire. Once you have them, you treat them like family and encourage them to add to that family by referring their friends and family. This sets in motion a cycle of abundance that will guarantee sustainable growth.

There are a few great examples of this theory, but I want to mention the World's Toughest Race Eco-Challenge, Fiji. It was a fantastic race held in Fiji that attracted 60 or so of the best four-man (and woman) teams from across the globe to compete for the title of the world's best adventure racer. This race was held over several days, and Netflix made a 10-episode TV series chronicling the event. The winning team from New Zealand came in at 141 hours and 23 minutes.

That is almost six full days out in the ocean, jungle, rivers, and mountains, grinding it out physically on makeshift kayaks, mountain bikes, and good old-fashioned feet. So why in the world am I bringing this race up in a medical practice management book? Well, it is just about the perfect example of the theory of "if you are not first, you're last," and why it is SO important for you to understand and practice this principle.

Let me explain based on the events that transpired in the race. At the beginning of the race, the winning team immediately capsized their boat in the river they were in. They didn't even make it to open water before their entire team was in the drink. However, once they got back on the boat, they immediately returned to the front of the pack, navigated the open ocean, and made it to their first big checkpoint. The two other leading teams had a much different checkpoint. One of them had a teammate from Oregon go into heat stroke and cause them to be stopped at the checkpoint until he was able to continue (they finished 40 hours behind Team New Zealand), and the other team took a wrong turn in the river and got lost, costing them about 2 hours to the checkpoint. As the race continued, the course wound up in a river canyon. This is where things got interesting. Team New Zealand navigated this canyon easily and moved on to the next checkpoint. However, a massive thunderstorm erupted and caused the canyon to flood. Team Estonia was hanging on to the side of the canyon and wound up stuck in a terrible position for hours. The race was stopped for anyone who had yet to pass the canyon. Team New Zealand didn't care at all. That was in their past. So the next big help they got was on the mountain bike stage. They were able to ride their bike on relatively easy dirt roads and had little trouble navigating this part of the race. However, due to the constant rain the others endured, the roads were damn near impassable on the bikes. Some teams even had to walk through the mud and carry their bikes due to the immense amount of mud on the roads.

As the race continued, Team New Zealand had to climb a beautiful waterfall in daylight, making it MUCH easier than the other teams who had no choice but to climb in the middle of the night. To top this off, they also had to wade in icy water above the waterfall, which caused many teams to quit. Participants were getting hypothermia due to being submerged in the water in the middle of the night vs. in the middle of the day. Time and time again, Team New Zealand avoided

MUCH harsher conditions from the weather and terrain simply because they were out in front. Nothing else was different other than that they had gotten ahead early and then capitalized big time on the theory that "if you are not first, you're last."

Please remember this when you are putting together your marketing campaigns.

Marketing Tips to Remember

- When you are ramping up your marketing, it is essential to remember that you do not want to have the phones ringing until you are fully prepared to start delivering the services. This may result in a short lag between being prepared and having the first patient come in. Still, you will be far better off in that position than being unable to provide services and potentially starting with a negative impression. For example, to ensure a successful start, it is essential to establish certain processes beforehand. These include having a proficient and focused phone receptionist to handle live calls, implementing tracking phone numbers to monitor all marketing channels, and recording and reviewing all incoming calls using our comprehensive 15 point questionnaire. These measures will help us achieve our goals effectively.

- As a clinic owner, taking control of your messaging and branding is essential. When seeking advice, staying true to your mission and values is crucial. Don't let anyone try to influence you to stray from what you believe in. Remember that your brand is a representation of who you are and what you stand for, so make sure that your messaging aligns.

- Quantity invariably beats quality. I cannot stress enough the importance of being everywhere or appearing as if you are everywhere. You want to create top-of-mind awareness in your community. Top-of-mind awareness is a measure of how high a brand ranks in the consciousness of consumers. It refers to the first brand that comes to mind when consumers think of a certain product category or industry. Being top-of-mind is a crucial component of consumer purchasing behavior. If your brand or product is the first consumers think of, consumers are more likely to buy it or choose you when the need arises. It would help if you continuously were thinking of how I can be top of mind in my community. What can I do today to raise my awareness? The more you do to make yourself known, the more you will reach top-of-mind awareness. You should be stalking your neighbor in their bushes. For example: who do you remember on the radio? The jingle you hear every hour on the hour on the radio, or the guy you see in one commercial every week on TV? While you want your message and branding to be integrated into your marketing, you can't allow perfectionism to delay you from getting it out into the world, and you may have to make a concession or two when it comes to the little things that may not line up perfectly.

John's Example

Dr. Keller is one of my clients in a small town in North Carolina. He owns a small, medically integrated physical medicine practice. The clinic sees about 100 patients a week and generates about 50k monthly, but it is growing rapidly. The goal for this office is 240k a month, so there is a long way to go, but it was only doing 15k six months ago. Why was he performing so poorly, considering he has been in practice for ten years and has a big, beautiful building in the middle of town?

Dr. Keller loves real estate and is a part-time developer. He also only works about 22 hours a week in his office. One of the first things we did was turn on some new creative to the newspaper. Dr. Keller came to me wondering why the newspaper ads were not bringing in more phone calls. His exact words were, "What the hell?" I looked at the situation and found that the newspaper had run an out-of-date ad copy with the wrong phone number.

The following week we turned on call tracking metrics and double-checked the copy before approving it. Lo and behold, we noticed the same patterns seen everywhere else in the country. Potential patients do call, but it is often during hours when the staff is not there to answer calls. They rarely leave voicemails, so when they call at 7:30 am, if you don't have a tracking system, you cannot know they called. The next issue we found came about through internal auditing of the calls themselves. I will never forget this scene. It was a Tuesday morning, and between calls with my clients, I listened to three new patient calls while Dr. Keller was at the office doing the same thing. As I listened, all I could think of was that I had never heard any staff at my clinics handle calls so badly. The scores were below 10 in the auditing chart, which runs on a scale from 0-74. I had my business partner, Heather, grade it, and she gave them 0s. Right before I got on my next client call, Dr. Keller sent me a text that read, "Just listened in on the new patient calls from yesterday. What the f***?" with about ten red-faced angry emojis following.

It was awful, but the worst part of what we heard was that she was creating massive objections on the phone regarding insurance, time, distance, and clinic availability. Mind you, Dr. Keller had been doing no marketing, training on how to handle calls, or auditing to track and score new patient calls. Does this make Dr. Keller:

> A. A bad businessman
> B. An idiot
> C. Lazy
> D. All of the above

The answer is E. None of the above. He is successful at developing real estate, highly intelligent and intuitive, and never stops moving all day.

The issue at hand is threefold. 1. He never took the time to market properly and implement systems. 2. He was too distracted by his other ventures to put a lot of intention on the clinic. And 3. He never did the proper amount of training and never had follow-up systems in place. He is now thriving and about three months away from removing himself from active practice thanks to the systems we implemented, which is precisely what I am discussing in this book.

This brief scenario serves as a prime example of the negative consequences that can arise from a lack of comprehension regarding the inner workings of a business. Specifically, it highlights deficiencies in both advertising strategies and employee training, two crucial areas that require attention.

Ask yourself this:

What do you want to create and convey with your content and message?

1. Who your avatar patient is
2. Why they should buy your services
3. Why they should buy from you now
4. What are the benefits of working with you?

The great news is that within this space, numerous agencies already have most of the answers. I am happy to connect you with any of the agencies I know well and who would be well-versed in what is needed to maximize your success with your particular profit vertical. Please email me to discuss what you need and who can help you.

The strategy I strongly recommend you NOT do this on your own. Let the experts handle it and hire a 1099 employee to handle your ads, track follow-up, and audit all of the working pieces of your marketing campaigns, such as:

- Newspaper Content
- Radio Ads
- Sales Funnels
- Social Media
- YouTube
- Google

Make sure going forward that you remember this quote from Grant Cardone. "The best product never, ever beats the best KNOWN product."

You may be the best Functional Medicine provider in the state, but if no one knows you are there, who cares?

We have found that one of the most effective and highest return on investment comes from doing community outreach programs. **Community Outreach** is an activity of educating a group about specific conditions and its treatment options. For us, outreach programs are seminars we offer to the public on specific health conditions we treat. We have several programs in place that have proven to be successful. Contact us for a list if you are interested in purchasing any of our programs.

The first thing in the process is to decide which program you will be doing. Then determine the location. The location should be a restaurant or hotel meeting room. Dinner workshops at a restaurant work best. At a dinner workshop, choose a restaurant with a private meeting room and provide the meal for the attendees. We suggest selecting a restaurant with a buffet so attendees can help themselves. It makes service much faster. (Try to find a pharmaceutical rep, supply rep for the service you are promoting, or imaging center to pick up the cost of the meal)
The programs should be advertised to the public using local newspapers, social media, or other media. We invite interested parties to attend a workshop. We then provide a 20-40 minute presentation on the condition, diagnosis, and treatment options. We sign up interested individuals for a consultation. (The consultation is **not** free)

It is best to advertise for no more than 2 weeks before the date of the program. Promoting further out has yet to be proven more effective and only seems to run up the cost. Sample Ads are available. The ad should be run on the 2 most read days of circulation for the print media of choice. You can get this information from the paper. For the best success with digital marketing, we have companies we can recommend.

The ad should give people a number to call to RSVP. (The front desk should be trained on proper phone script and scheduling.) Most meeting rooms will hold a limited number of participants. It is best to limit the group to a maximum of 50 attendees. Above 50 it is more difficult to control the room, answer questions, and schedule people for consultations. If you have more than 50 interested, hold a second meeting immediately after or schedule another date within one week.

The front desk should keep a running list of the individuals that call along with the name, contact phone number and name of any guest who will be attending with them. (A sample of the RSVP log is provided here.) Most people who come will bring someone with them to the meeting. Therefore you can anticipate that half of the people who show up will be viable candidates. Make sure that each person who calls knows the date, time and directions to the program.

A couple of days before the program, someone should call each attendee to confirm their attendance and to remind them of the location. Ensure they have directions and remind them to show up 15 minutes early to get signed in. The day before the meeting, contact the meeting place and confirm the number of attendees. Arrange for audio-visual equipment. The programs are in a PowerPoint presentation format so we will need a projector and a screen. Some meeting places will have a screen.

Be sure to have marketing information to hand out to the attendees about the clinic and about the procedure or services that you offer. We suggest you hand these out as people sign in. Putting them on the table tends to waste some of the materials. Also, always have a primary health survey at every seat with a pen so they can fill it out before the lecture. This will give you their basic demographics and an idea of their primary area of concern. Finally, You can use this info to build a database of future leads to market in case they are not ready to come and get the services you offer. Make sure one of your staff is there to collect the surveys before food service. Remember- as stated above- do a buffet, it is easier.

On the day of the meeting, make sure to have name tags. Purchase name tags from the office supply store. Print out a copy of the physician's schedule for one week. Do this before leaving for the program. You will use this schedule to book patients at the end of the program. Only print out for one week as statistics show the further out the appointment, the lower the probability a person will keep the appointment. People have a higher show rate when everything is fresh on their minds.

Upon arrival, have attendees sign in and give them a name tag. Name tags should be used so we can keep up with who is with our group.

Have one of the greeters introduce the speaker (you) and make sure she gives a short bio of your schooling, years in practice, etc. Finally, make sure she reminds the people attending that due to HIPPA, all questions need to be held until the end and will be addressed in a one-on-one after the lecture is over. Answering all their questions now is not the goal. Disseminating information and showing them you may have a solution to their health care problem is so stick to the plan.

Now- I want to ensure we cover some of the basics and the differences between the professionals and the amateurs in this space. If this system is done correctly, it will bring you the most new business and consistent revenue from all the other marketing you do for your practice. (Greatest return on investment ROI.) Yes, it is a little more labor-intensive and time-consuming, but it is also your best strategy for sustained growth.

Here is a rundown of the overall protocols and what is required to make this work. Remember- just running postcards or Facebook ads and then sitting back and printing money is a pipe dream. This system requires some planning and setup, but it gets easier and more streamlined after you have done a few.

Think about and map out all these protocols before running this outreach seminar. You will do much better if all of these are in place and everyone involved is trained and queued in on the processes.

1. Care plans for the patients
2. Sales Cycles and financial handles/ financing options
3. Objection handles.
4. Recall protocol
5. Role-play the seminar
6. Staff responsibilities write-ups- before and after.
7. Which stats will be tracked for the workshop, and who is responsible?
8. Phone call tracking
9. Phone scripting and training.
10. Checklists
11. The ideal scene for this system with specific goals and targets.
12. Bonus structure for staff.
13. Scheduling for various times and around holidays.
14. Restaurant location and menu.

It sounds like a lot of work. But you can't take the elevator to the top of the mountain. You have to climb it, and I promise that after doing 60-70 events a year for over a decade, this system is by far your best option to scale your practice.

If you want help with this system, reach out. I have some resources to help guide you and can also come and teach you or your staff the community outreach system.

As I have said before - the first hat you wear as a business owner is that of a marketer. If anyone asks, you should identify yourself as a marketer, and your focus should ALWAYS be on marketing because if you do not have patients, you do not have a business!!
LETS GO!

Chapter 4

Mistake #4

Not Keeping Track of and Understanding

The Importance of Statistics

What is the connection between climbing Kilimanjaro and your statistics? Let me tell you a little story. When I decided to tackle the seven summits as a life goal, I did so only with the intention for it to be a goal so big that my focus was on something other than the end result. I only wanted to enjoy the journey. That journey has taught me many lessons that can be applied to life, business, and medical practice.

Hiking big mountains has its share of risks, the most obvious of which is falling off. Others include freezing, snow blindness, and altitude sickness, to name a few. There is some mitigated risk involved, and there are a few correlations with mountain climbing in relation to your business and how you measure gains, losses, wins, and setbacks. On a mountain, small mistakes can carry significant consequences. I want to hammer this home because properly assessing the journey is critical to your overall business health.

I want to begin with what a climb looks like and what a successful outcome entails, all the things you must account for and pay attention to on a mountain.

First, you must be physically prepared. You must train for what you are about to undergo to handle the strain. As such, you'd to track your daily workouts, including calories burned, calories consumed, and any weight loss or gain. You must purchase the appropriate gear for the environment and ensure everything is in order. While on the mountain, you have to be hyper-aware of the weather, the pace at which you are moving, whether or not you are navigating correctly, whether you have lost anything, how many calories and how much water you are consuming, etc., etc., etc.... These statistics are critical to hitting your target (the summit) and for your survival. Making the right decisions at the right time based on the information you have at your disposal can mean life or death. The exact process applies to the survival of your business. You must train to be prepared for your business journey. You have to make sound decisions from accurate Key Performance Indicators (KPIs) on a week-to-week and month-to-month basis. Without training and statistics in place, it is almost impossible to reach your goal.

Metrics, Statistics, Key Performance Indicators.

One of the many pieces of information you must be mindful of is your statistics. How do you keep your stats? What program do you use to track your metrics? The responses I usually get are either Google Sheets or Excel. However, these are rarely up-to-date or accurate. If you are not tracking stats or keeping up with them daily, how do you know what to do or even what problems you might have? Not monitoring our stats leads to massive confusion, which leads to fear, which is the true underlying condition that causes you to avoid watching the stats altogether. If you do not actively follow your metrics weekly, you will constantly be flying by the seat of your pants and always make bad, or at the bare minimum, under informed decisions. Even the most intelligent humans and business owners make piss-poor decisions all the time and run their clinics with a whack-a-mole strategy until they are so exhausted they throw their hands up and either quit or get so desperate they finally hire a consultant to help. I was there early on in my career and understood the frustration.

Not tracking statistics and following metrics is the source of the Sunday Night Blues I've mentioned previously. It's Sunday evening, and instead of relaxing with your family and enjoying what's left of your weekend, you are stressed out with no idea of how many new patients you will have or trying to figure out how you will pay the light bill and payroll.

Tracking statistics is key to measuring and improving organizational performance. They provide valuable insights into the health and efficiency of your clinic and enable effective decision-making. By identifying trends and measuring progress, statistics can pinpoint areas that require improvement. Analyzing statistics helps identify and resolve obstacles hindering progress towards goals. Specific statistical targets and metrics ensure that your practice is moving towards its goals. They are used to manage all aspects of your organization, including finances, new patients, patient visits, and employee performance. Regularly tracking statistics improves efficiency, productivity, and overall success.

You need to incorporate a statistics tracking system. One of the ones I have used that has been out a long time and is incredibly easy is Condition Formulas. Some of the most important statistics to track and manage using these statistics are:

- New Patients
- Patient Visits
- Total amount of money billed out for services provided
- Total Money Collected
- New Patient Calls
- Reactivations
- ROIS based on marketing and phone system
- All profit verticals broke down

I am going to break down the basics and work through the overall system. First, you need some way to track your metrics daily, weekly, and monthly even if you are not using it correctly or at all at the moment. If not, there are numerous cheap software options out there, and you need to pick one that fits your budget and offers the features you need. Remember that your

EMR system will not cut it for all the stats. We have a system that is less expensive and that will assist you. Contact my office for more details.

The second thing to consider is that every clinic is different regarding its profit verticals, and some clinics assign other metrics to be tracked. A Profit Vertical analysis analyzes an income statement by comparing all line items to the revenue or overall sales number. In a vertical analysis, the revenue or sales number is 100%, and all other line items are a percentage of sales.

A profit center is a department or area within a company that contributes to the company's revenue and profits. Profit centers are responsible for generating revenue and incurring costs for the business. Examples of profit centers include sales, production, and service. The main goal of a profit center is to maximize profits and contribute to the overall profitability of the business.)

An example for practice in physical medicine, and procedures like body contouring, Botox, and laser facelifts for the aesthetics groups. You have to keep them separated inside the office so you can track their stats more easily and more efficiently. Examples would include weight loss, neuropathy, spinal decompression, large joint injections

One of the clearest examples of a vertical is a client who realized after we cleaned up her stats and organized them that she was not making any profit in doing IV therapy in her office. IVs are great, but by the time she paid for the Facebook ads, the supplies, and the staff involved, she only earned around $3,000 a month in profit while spending almost 30 percent of the week's time doing the procedures. Once she realized this and stopped offering them, her collection on her other verticals tripled because we diverted her IV marketing budget to hormone replacement/weight loss.

First, you must decide what statistics should be tracked or what profit verticals. Then, who is responsible for compiling the data. You need to map out who is responsible for which metrics for accountability purposes. Once you have the data, it must be in a visual graph format. With this information, you will take a set of actions based on the condition of those statistics. I will give examples of each shortly, but if a metric is going up, you take specific steps. If it is going down, you do something else. If it is staying the same, that would be considered going down. If it is crashing, you handle that in a very specific manner.

When managing using statistics and statistical trends, you should think of your stats like a snapshot and the graphical trends as if it is a movie. To manage a business by statistics, you first need to determine the most important statistics to track and then learn how to interpret data and then what to do with it.

Tracking
The questions you need to answer with the metrics you are using are:

1. What do you track?
2. Who tracks what?
3. How do you interpret the data
4. What do YOU do with the data?
5. How are they held accountable (weekly office meetings with reports)?

Then, what are the basic statistics you should track weekly:

1. Number of new patients
2. Number of overall patient visits
3. Advertising dollars spent

4. Number of new patient phone calls
5. Number of new patient appointments
6. Number of missed or rescheduled new patients
7. Number of sign-ups
8. Total Services Billed out
9. Total collections
10. Collections by profit vertical
11. Number of procedures by provider, broken down by different profit verticals

The final piece of this puzzle is handling the numbers based on trends. Managing by statistics involves using specific data you obtain from your practice and applying statistical analysis to guide your management decisions for each area. You will compile data daily for the things in the clinic that are most important to growth and success. Items include new patients, patient visits, total billed, total collected, profit, and return on investment for various programs. Anything that you want to grow or improve must be tracked.

You should look at your number daily, weekly, and monthly; however, most of your decisions will be made using weekly trends. Weekly trends smooth out the intrinsic daily variability in the data and provide a more stable trend. Daily data points can be heavily influenced by random fluctuations, noise, or anomalies such as weekends, holidays, weather, or special events that do not accurately reflect the underlying trends. By grouping the data into weekly intervals, you reduce the impact of these short-term fluctuations and identify more stable patterns. Weekly trends strike a balance between short-term responsiveness, allowing you to capture relatively recent changes and trends while avoiding the potential pitfalls of overreacting to short-term fluctuations. Likewise, monthly trends are also significant but can cause you to be too slow to react in many cases. That is why most stats are focused on weekly.

When managing by statistics, visual graphs are needed to get a clear understanding to make assessments of trends and patterns that help you make informed decisions. When analyzing data, we look for trends. Three types of trends can be observed: upward, downward, and no change.

Upward Trend:
An upward trend occurs when the data points consistently increase over time. This indicates positive growth or improvement in the measured variable. For example, if the collections graph shows increasing

collections week over week, it suggests that the practice is growing. The significance of an upward trend is that it provides evidence of progress and success. This trend is a positive outcome, and you should continue expanding current strategies to further capitalize on the growth. You do this by identifying the factors contributing to the upward trend and taking action to reinforce them.

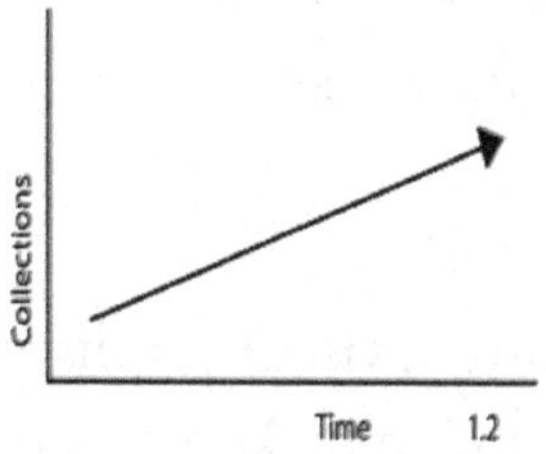

Believe it or not, this is the most dangerous trend of all. This is where almost everyone (myself included back in the day) makes the biggest financial mistakes that destroy their businesses. When you see an upward trend happening with one of your stats, you need to:

a. Economize your bills to improve your cash flow

    b. Put those funds into your advertising budget
    c. Don't change what you are doing.
    d. Keep up with weekly staff meetings and, again, find where you can be a more effective leader and improve communication

Here is why this trend is dangerous. Take, for example, Dr. Mark. He started a men's health practice in Montana. His practice took off, and the collections ramped to over 200k monthly. His overhead was very low because it was patients with biologics and hormones. He was spending about 10k on marketing, and his payroll was around 15k. He owned the building and rented out other suites, so he had no rent. He was spending about 20k a month on the biologic products, so when it was all said and done, the overhead ended up being around 50k.

Here is what usually happens in this scenario and also in this case. Dr. Mark started taking trips out of town and then bought a 911. He purchased a ranch outside of town with a barn to house hypothetical animals. He added about 25k per month in extra bills. The two things he needed to do, which were critical at this point, don't change what he was doing that got him to that point, economizing to get out of debt, and protecting his money.

The end of the year rolled around, and things went from bad to worse. Not only did he owe over 300k in taxes, he had to have a quadruple bypass surgery that did not go well. The government placed a large lien on the practice, and he was in severe financial trouble.

When your stats are in an upward trend, you have to make sure no matter what, you protect whatever it is that got it there in the first place. Maybe it's not your advertising that got it there, the new case manager you hired, or that the new patient numbers have exploded, but whatever it is that created the stat rocking, find it and protect it.

If the stat that is rising is the money coming into the practice, DO NOT BUY ANYTHING or take on any new debt. For the love of God, do not buy a new piece of equipment for 200k in some "scheme" to avoid paying taxes. That devalues your company, making it harder to sell while increasing the need to ramp up production. There is just no need for it.

If you need to spend money, which happens, do it to increase your capacity to deliver services and make it easier and faster to provide them. This is NOT the same as buying a shiny new toy. You may have legitimate things that must be purchased, repaired, or upgraded. You may need to add a sink in a room, buy a new centrifuge, tear down a wall, add a new marketing vertical, or put in a new phone system. These things will increase your ceiling of capacity and allow you to grow.

Downward Trend:

A downward trend is the opposite of an upward trend. It signifies a consistent decrease in the data points over time.

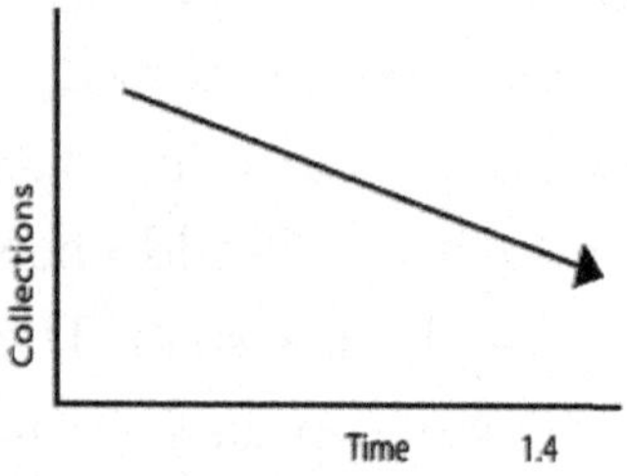

This could indicate a decline in performance or a problem that needs attention. For instance, collections show a decreasing trend over a week. It could suggest a problem in the billing department or that the front desk is not collecting at the time of service. The significance of a downward trend is that it alerts you to potential issues that need to be addressed much quicker than would be typically noticed and allows for swift action. The downward trend alerts you to investigate the causes behind the decline and take corrective measures to reverse the trend. This may involve identifying and resolving underlying problems, adjusting strategies, or implementing changes to improve performance.

When you find a down statistic, you need to take immediate and massive action to bring the stat back to an upward trend. You must analyze what changed that caused the stat to go down and take corrective action. It could be a holiday last week, and you were closed one day, or a new front desk person is not collecting at the time of service, so training needs to be done, etc.

No Change:

A situation with no significant change in the data points over time represents a flat or stable trend.

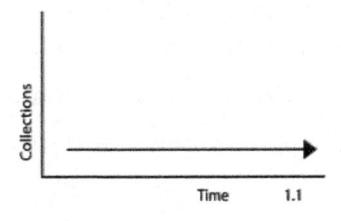

Graph: Collections vs. Time, showing a flat horizontal line. Labeled 1.1

This means that the variable being measured has remained relatively constant. The significance of no change should be a sense of stability and predictability, which is partially correct. However, since there is no such thing as a constant, things are constantly changing, which ultimately means things are either getting better or worse; Therefore, no change would indicate an area of concern. It prompts you to look for and analyze the factors contributing to the lack of change. You will need to determine where there are opportunities for improvement and get them implemented.

Keep in mind that some trends are directly influence by other trends so it is important to assess all the areas being managed by statistics

In summary, visual graphs are valuable tools for managing by statistics as they allow you to observe and interpret trends in the data. Upward trends indicate positive growth; downward trends and no change highlight issues that need addressing. Understanding these trends and their significance helps you and your managers make informed decisions and take appropriate actions to drive organizational success.

One final piece I want to add to this chapter is the system we use to manage staff and hold them accountable by their statistics. The system has three essential parts: staff owning their key stats, monitoring them using the condition formulas, and finally, presenting them at the weekly production meeting.

Let's demonstrate the system here using the front desk position using a couple of stats and explain how you would run this system in your office to increase accountability and production. This will be a basic rundown of this system, and we will start with using two stats that the front desk should keep track of in any practice. Once you see the basics, you can apply this to any other post and add any stats as you see fit for that position. However, we recommend only giving each post a few stats. If you overwhelm them with ten different stats, the staff member will get paralyzed.

- Step 1. Figure out the stats you want the staff member responsible for in their day-to-day activities. In our example, we use the front desk position and the two stats of the number of new patients and the number of patient visits the office saw that day. Again, the front desk will have more than just these two stats, but this is a basic example, and you can add the stats as you see fit.

You train the staff member that she is responsible for these two stats and then train them where to store the stats (there are many software out there you can buy, but your EMR will have the ability to track these basic numbers).

- Step 2. You train them on how to look at the trends using the formulas we provided above so they can understand where those numbers are - *and what the next course of action should be based on that condition.* This is a relatively straightforward process and should be easy for them to pick up on after a couple of weeks. If your staff member is having a hard time finding their stats and interpreting the data, you have made a bad decision in the hiring process.

- Step 3. Once a week, you should have a production meeting where they present the stats they are accountable for *AND* present the next steps that should be taken to improve them.

So, let's do a quick overview and give an example. The front desk receptionist has kept up with her stats all week, inputting them into whatever system is used to track the business stats. She takes five minutes to go back and compare the stats to the previous four weeks and sees a significant downturn in the new patient numbers for the week, and it is a part of a more significant trend that the overall new patient numbers have been falling for a month. She presents her stats and findings at the weekly production meeting. Because of her training, she knows to look for the reasons for the decline, and more importantly, *you have been made aware of the issue, and you can now openly handle it with engaged staff and map out the solution.* So- as the owner, you look at why the numbers could be dropping. First, ask the marketing director if anything changes with the "pull" from the marketing, aka- is the marketing still consistently making the phone ring? Has the phone receptionist turned in her scoring sheets from the new patient phone calls? If so, has anyone audited the actual calls? Is the patient being called the night before to confirm their appt? What matters is 1, you have identified the problem, and 2, you and your staff know where to find the SOLUTION.

This system is one of the most important things you can do for your business. I strongly recommend you implement this in your office immediately.

Bonus Section

Let's discuss how and what the bonus system should look like in your practice, and then we will focus on a few guidelines and examples. Bonuses can be highly motivating but also demotivating if the system is mishandled. That said, if done correctly, it can increase compliance, production, and morale, and I recommend having a solid bonus system in place.

Before I get into the bonus system, I would like to talk to you about two important concepts that will help you understand the importance of the bonus system and staff in general.

1. You cannot build a large company based on "satisfied customers."
2. The law of differentiation. In basic terms, it states that the greater the value you give to a customer (patient), the lower the price resistance. In other words, the more exceptional customer service you provide, the less price matters to the patient.

Let me explain these two concepts briefly, and then we will focus on the bonuses.

You have to think about being so good at delivering an exceptional customer experience that you create a scene where there is you and everyone else. The extreme differentiation in customer experience separates the "satisfied customer" from the "raving fans" customer. Customers believe what they "experience," not what you say.

Let's dig into this with some truly insane numbers run by an extensive survey conducted by the company SMG (similar to JD Power and associates) focusing on the differences in how customers see a business and how the business owner sees their business. The survey asked a simple question: Rate your last experience with a business where you received a service and paid for it.

- Seventy-nine percent of customers said their last experience was average or below average.
- Only THREE percent said it was exceptional. Let's reframe this in another way. There are two groups of small businesses out there. The ninety-seven percent who suck at what they do. And three percent who have it together and

perform at an exceptional level. Be honest; where do you stand? It's ok, we can fix it.

Now, Let's flip the script. SMG then asked the business owners to rate themselves on their level of customer service. Their response?

- Eighty percent said they were exceptional. Eight in ten owners said they were awesome at delivering extraordinary service.
- No owners admitted to giving "bad" customer service even though forty-one percent of the customers rated it that way. Let that sink in for a minute.

There are so many layers to this poor self-awareness and blindness from the owners. They think; Well, as long as I am not getting any complaints and the bills are being paid, then we must be doing something right. The owner's inability to see the actual scene indicates 1. They cannot see the problem, so they never fix it, and 2. Operate under the false assumption they are providing excellent customer service when they are not.

Remember this: It is not crowded at the top. When you are exceptional at the patient experience, you will never have a cash flow problem. Your excellent culture and how you make the patients *FEEL* are why your competition does not matter. You don't have any real outside competitors if you can provide that experience level. The only real competition is you- and your acceptance of average being the standard in your business. Stop the self-inflicted wounds now! A sound bonus system is one way to help keep your staff focused on their target and motivate them to deliver the experience.

Now that I got my little rant out of the way, let's get back to the bonus system, and how you build the system in such a way the staff stays motivated to keep delivering exceptional service.
Let's build a foundation for the bonus system and lay out a few rules.

1. Giving bonuses for just doing their job is stupid. We are not giving out participation trophies. In business, there are winners and losers. We are not giving out spiffs or cash so that you can keep an entitled employee happy. Remember, as desperation rises, standards fall. Do not get desperate with your employees. They are on your clock, so do not reward (or

accept) average performance. Just getting by is not how we roll. They get bonuses when they go above and beyond their standard work stats.

2. Do NOT set your benchmarks for your goals so low that they always hit them, and then expect a hand-out. You are not the morons at the federal government and do not have a printing press in your backyard to print money. Always keep the standards high. Keep YOUR standards high first, and expect the same from everyone else on the team. DO not bonus the staff just because they are doing a job or wearing a hat you choose not to do yourself. That is poor leadership.

3. Always remember to train them very well on their key activities that lead to them receiving a bonus. They should never come back to you and say something to the effect, "Well, I have not even been trained on that system. How do you expect me to hit that target without understanding what to do to get there"? This one seems crazy to read- but we see it all the time.

4. Do not set goals too crazy high from the beginning. Let's say you are collecting 40k a month, and then you sit the team down for a meeting and say - I will give you all 1000 bucks if we hit 100k this month. What do you think they will say? They probably won't say anything to your face. They will laugh and make fun of you later.

5. Never give out bonuses that are meant for someone else. I am saying, DO NOT give everyone in the office the same bonus when one or two key players did most of the work. It will build resentment in the all-star players. It will make the average employees even MORE average than they already are and more entitled in their thinking while sitting on their phones watching tik tok videos sucking their thumbs like little whiny babies- on your clock.

A staff member should only be bonused on a stat or metric they can control or affect. Here are some basic examples of what a possible bonus system could look like in your practice. Let's go through a basic example first.

Example 1. The new phone receptionist has been trained on the call tracking system and the auditing score sheets. She has gone through several role-play sessions with the office manager and is ready to start answering the phones live. We have made sure we are setting her up for success. You sit her down and review the numbers for the number of inbound and outbound calls the practice receives weekly. She understands that, on average, you get fifteen new patient calls a week, and eight new patients come in on any given week. It is her job to *at least keep the numbers the same.* However, If she is solid at her post and the number increases, you will give her an extra 10 dollars per new patient walk-in. So usually, they will find more ways to contact old patients, make sure to be on point and not be distracted during calls, etc. Suddenly, the new patient numbers go up to twelve a week, and they earn an extra 40 bucks a week doing their job and doing it well. If she starts an outreach campaign, she can also be bonused for old follow-up patients. She might even be bonuses on overall collections. That is up to you. Any stat they are responsible for and trained to do in your practice should have a bonus added.

Example 2. This bonus will go to whoever holds the marketing post. Let's set the scene two ways. One, they have come on board new and are starting from scratch on the post. Like the scenario above, we have set them up for success through massive training and role-playing. Their job is to monitor the new patient call numbers on the call tracking metrics website to determine which marketing pieces are giving the best returns on the ad spend. Remember- all marketing pieces have a tracking number so we can understand what is going on with the marketing.

On top of that, they have to coordinate with the office manager and case manager weekly which piece of marketing is giving the best value based on the type of patient coming in (for example, Facebook ads may be making the phone ring off the hook and look good on the surface but when you dig in you see there are a ton of no shows and the ones who schedule don't have a pot to piss in or a window to throw it out). This is the job they get paid to do. However, let's say you add the lecture series to the current marketing plan. Now, the marketing director has a way to get a solid bonus. You can bonus them on the number of people who attend the lecture. Let's say 30 bucks if more than 15 potential new patients show. Fifty dollars if more than 25 show up for the event. It is your system, so you decide. Hopefully, you can see the difference. The person should not get rewarded for doing their job but for going above and beyond and doing things past just doing the day-to-day that you already pay them for in the office.

These are just a couple of basics. When you first implement a practice-wide bonus system, it can be daunting and confusing. Still, it can really help ramp up production and motivate the staff to focus on exceptional patient satisfaction. If you need help with the entire system, email me. We can set them up for your employees based on the posts they hold in the organization.

Chapter 5

Mistake Number 5

Not Understanding the Difference Between Being Busy and Being Productive

<u>Being Busy vs. Being Productive, A Tale of Two Grandparents:</u>

I have a story to share with you to stress how important it is to design every activity you and your staff undergo during a work week to focus on the main targets you have set for your business. When I was about 13 years old, my mom and adoptive father divorced, causing an already dire financial situation to go from bad to worse. One weekend on my summer break before 9th grade, my grandfather decided he would give me a way to earn some much-needed cash for the household. Grandpa was an uneducated man who dropped out of high school and went straight to work in the trucking industry. He was able to retire well and paid cash for his dream home away from civilization in Ceasar's Head at the entrance to Jones Gap State Park in upstate South Carolina. It lies between Brevard, NC, and Greenville, SC, which are far more densely populated than in the

1980s when this story takes place. Back in my day (I am officially old enough to say that now), that entire area was considered just about as far out in the sticks as you can get. Side note: if you ever happen to be down that way, I assure you the chili dogs at the gas station by the entrance to Jones Gap State Park are the best you'll ever find. But I digress... I hope you can take a moment to visualize driving past Jones Gap down a country road on a sunny summer day. You pass a small volunteer fire station on your right and watch for the old dance hall. Behind the dance hall is a river. Across the rivers lies the long white house where I was taught the only lesson I never needed in the difference between being busy and being productive.

My Grandpa Tommy approached me that summer to let me know that he wanted a road cut from his land up around the nearby pond and to connect it to an old logging road that led to the main road by the river. My mom and I were flat broke, so I agreed to help with the project despite being only thirteen and having limited experience in urban planning and DOT work. The first problem was that there was no way this road would ever be finished. For starters, the road was going straight off the side of a very steep incline, and no engineer worth a damn would ever have designed it; it was so steep that if any idiot did build that road, it would have washed out quickly and completely. The second problem is that it would have led to a small road with three houses on it, which had not changed in thirty-four years, and it would have created a circle about one mile in diameter.

Granted, I didn't care about any of that. I was getting paid three dollars an hour, which meant something back then. Day after day, I showed up with my saw and wheelbarrow, cut trees, moved rocks, and shoveled dirt. About four days of hard work later, I had completed about thirty feet of Interstate Skidmore. That fantastic little piece of engineering is a bit overgrown, but that area I cleared for the big machines to drop asphalt remains by the pond, heading straight to nowhere to this very day.

About a year later, my mother was hospitalized for what would be the first of many stomach surgeries. Grandpa Tommy demanded I quit the ninth grade, drop out of high school like he did, and go to work. I refused, and our relationship was never the same. He was a really good guy with values that were no longer acceptable for the current times and a misguided understanding of what it meant to be busy vs. productive. His lesson was obviously that hard work pays off, and nobody should get anything for free. I know he didn't want that extension of the I-20 through his backyard, and he was finding a way to emphasize that I was "earning" the hundred dollars I made that week (with an extra 20 thrown in because I didn't quit). In fairness to him, I felt downright loaded with that kind of money in my pocket. I felt a sense of accomplishment even if I did fall about 5,250 feet short of my one mile.

Looking back, what did I actually accomplish? I was completely unproductive and came nowhere near completing the assigned task. Did I learn a fantastic life lesson? Yes. I learned: 1. I am definitely not cut out for manual labor, and 2. A massive difference exists between being busy all day and being on the production line and producing and doing the necessary daily tasks that need to be done to work toward your WIG (Wildly Important Goal).

The summer before the story above, I had an equally impactful experience with my other grandfather, B.F., that I will never forget. That set of grandparents also lived in a rural area and had about four acres of land. They let me cut the lower pasture on a riding lawn mower when I visited. It would take me about four hours to get the entire pasture cut back, and they would pay me twenty dollars for my efforts—five dollars an hour to ride around cutting grass. I enjoyed doing it while rocking out to my Sony Walkman (Foreigner was my jam). It was a pretty good deal, considering a year later, I entered a devil's bargain to build the Interstate 20 bypass for only three bucks an hour. Grandpa B.F. added an even bigger perk to this deal: As a twelve-year-old, I didn't care about health benefits or a 401K, but I loved golf. B.F. was a lefty like myself (although my handicap of thirty was a far stretch from his two). I loved playing with him and his old buddies. We couldn't afford the Furman University golf course, so we played the Summerset course on the side of Paris Mountain. Playing the game with B.F. and his friends was great, but I was especially partial to the free peanuts and R.C. Cola. He even let me drive the golf cart until I spun it out on a hill and scared the hell out of him.

You may wonder what this all has to do with your practice or the book's point. Well, pretty much everything! I loved and respected these men, and they taught me essential but different lessons about living my life. Grandpa Tommy taught me to work hard on a pipe dream without clear targets or vision. There was no real reason to be out there doing that task. It simply kept me busy wasting time to put a few dollars in my pocket. B.F. taught me to do what I loved and get paid well in a comfortable environment. I negotiated additional perks to chase my passions: salted peanuts, R.C. Cola, and taking the driver's seat in the golf cart.

The moral of these two stories is this: Do what you enjoy and are good at to make the money you need to find your true passion.

Your Practice Day, Chaos Theory, and a Huge Pile of Dinosaur Sh*t.

It may not make sense to you now, but as the name of this section implies, all three of these things are interconnected and come into play in practices day after day, week after week, month after month, and, unfortunately, year after year.

We'll start with Monday. You get your day started after a night of the Sunday Blues, which is that feeling that hits around 7 p.m. that either stresses you out about the number of patients you need, how you're going to make payroll, which employee has to be fired, and whether the advertising is going to work. Most of the weekend, you can stay busy enough to distract yourself from these intrusive thoughts, but as Sunday evening hits, it all starts pushing its way to the forefront of your mind.

It's also important to remember that becoming a better leader requires dedication and effort. While it can be tempting to spend all your free time binge-watching the latest Netflix dramas, the truth is that this won't do much to help you grow and develop as a leader. Instead, make a concerted effort to prioritize your personal growth and development in order to become the best leader you can be.

Now let's spend a moment talking about the focus of the practice day. **Here are the 5 basic tenets of a successful day. Remember this phrase:**

You will never get back what you lost today.

1. Prepare for work before you are at work. As a matter of fact- prepare for work the night before by getting the right amount of sleep and waking up early to get your mind right for the day.

   You never have to recover from a great start.

Do you start your day by meditating, exercising, journaling and aligning your attitude, or are you wasting time scrolling through Facebook, TikTok, or even worse Bumble? Do you rush to work at the last minute or arrive early and consistently? Your employees observe your behavior, and it sets the tone for the day. Your attitude and actions influence your staff, so you must lead by example to establish the expectations you have for them.

How do you develop and influence your attitude? Let me offer a few suggestions. It's essential to understand that our attitude towards life can determine our level of success and happiness. To begin with, it's crucial to identify negative thought patterns and replace them with positive ones. Practicing gratitude and focusing on the present can also help to shift one's attitude towards a more positive outlook. Additionally, surrounding oneself with positive and supportive people can have a significant impact on attitude. Lastly, setting achievable goals and celebrating small victories along the way can help to improve one's attitude and overall outlook on life.

Another way to accomplish this is to STACK good habits on top of each other. What does this mean? Research shows that if you want to start a new positive habit, let's say, meditation or journaling, you should add it to any of your other positive habits. An example could look like this- one of your good habits is working out in the morning before work, but you only have time for a shower and the trip to the office and nothing else. A good idea is to get up 15 minutes early and use that time to journal before you hit the gym. This could work in the opposite direction as well. Think about all the people you know who only smoke when they are drinking or binge eat only when they are watching TV (maybe it's you). My point is that we stack our bad habits just like we do the good ones.

Stacking positive habits on ones you already have will make doing the new habits much easier and get them ingrained in your brain faster, becoming a positive habit that prepares you for the day. The right attitude and mindset are more important than skills, knowledge, and talent.

> 2. Prepare for work while you are driving to work.

Mindless radio and television is an income suppressant- Zig Ziglar.

Listen to educational, motivating, or inspirational books or podcasts. Do not listen to the DJs on the radio and all their drama. When you hear the drama, you bring that crap to the office, and you can become the one spreading the drama to your staff and then to the patients.

If you feel like you need a hug and a nursing bottle every morning when you get to work, you are either doing the wrong job, don't have a productive morning routine to get your mind right, or both.

> 3. Have a plan and follow it.

It's important to have a plan and stick to it. This may seem like a straightforward step, but it's often overlooked. Make sure to tackle your most important tasks first and avoid distractions. Attack your priorities.

Do not attack the donuts! Protect your time at all costs and stay focused on your WIG (Wildly Important Goal). Don't reward being busy; instead, prioritize productivity. While this may appear to be a simple concept, it is frequently disregarded. To ensure that you are making the most of your time, it is vital to prioritize your most pressing responsibilities and avoid any potential distractions that could derail your progress. Always remember-

Do not reward busy. Only focus on production.

4. Adopt a servant leadership approach.

To be an effective leader, it is absolutely crucial that you prioritize the support and wellbeing of your staff. Act with intention and lead with compassion instead of solely focusing on yourself and your issues. By adopting a servant leadership approach, you can unlock a wealth of benefits that will help you to become a more effective and respected leader.

To help facilitate your personal growth and development as a leader, be sure to invest time in reading inspirational literature, listening to spiritual podcasts, and engaging in self-improvement activities.

These efforts can help you to expand your horizons, gain valuable insights, and develop a more nuanced and effective leadership style.

    5. Review the day and watch the tape.

This means at the end of the day take an inventory of the scene as it played out the way sports teams watch tape of their games. Ask yourself:

- What went right, what went wrong.
- How could you have performed better?
- How could you have been a better leader?
- Did you protect your time?
- Are you someone who inspires greatness or someone who gossips and talks to everyone about their personal problems?

We become so reliant upon our subconscious that we go on autopilot, starting with the drive-in and, once there, continue to do so instead of focusing on our WIG (Wildly Important Goal). If we do happen to start our day off on the right foot with a staff/sales meeting (which most don't), we focus on what is wrong. There is always an angry patient to deal with or some other problem. One of the most consistent and challenging things I dealt with on Monday mornings was my network computer systems. For some reason or another, they always decided to crash out over the weekend when updates were taking place. This happened at least once a month and left us with half a day of headaches until the IT guy down the block showed up to fix it. That and many other Gremlins just always seemed to pop up on Monday mornings to take our focus off what was important.

Reminds me of that scene from Jurassic Park where the chaos theorist Malcom gets out of the car and walks up to a mountain of dinosaur sh*t? Do not let your day get away from you and wind up driving home thinking about your day like that scene. Nothing but a big pile of sh*t!

How does this relate to running a medical practice? You start your day with nothingness, a blank slate filled with what you bring to the clinic as the owner and your habits, thoughts, expertise, and agenda. Way more often than not, instead of running a tight, well-oiled machine in which the staff is focused on the WIG and the one or two most important activities they should be focused on, what happens is a series of one distraction after another. Bad decisions are made because you aren't focusing on what's important. Dealing with upset patients or HR issues in the clinic is just an environment of uncontrolled chaos. At the end of the day, you were busy as hell with little to nothing to show for it, and for all intents and purposes, you are staring at "one big pile of shit." I'm confident that there is something in what I am saying to which you can relate. Maybe you're only staring at a small pile. You may have had a great week, month, or year. However, you will always be surrounded by controlled chaos unless you are completely focused on your WIG.

Planning your day (including your morning routine) and protecting your schedule and time while being hyper-focused on your key activities to drive your practice toward its goals is how you go from good to great and become the master of your craft versus simply chasing your passion. Again, I see this scene play out every day.

Amanda's Story (Part 1)

Let's talk about my client Amanda. Amanda is a Physician Assistant (PA) I consulted in Oklahoma.

Let's examine one of her days as repeated to me on a Tuesday morning and see if any of this nonsense is relatable to your office.

I asked her about the start of the week and inquired why I was not seeing any of her stats from Monday. Here is her response. I have heard this same response thousands of times, and I knew I was in for a whopper based on her tone. "Well, here is how my Monday went. First, I had to turn around and head back to the satellite office because my medical assistant (MA) had left a bunch of supplies there on Friday that we needed in the main office. That set me back 45 minutes. Then, the PA Casey had an emergency with her sick kid, and she had to skip her shift. Because of that, I was running around all day seeing her patients, and I had no time to get anything done. The worst part of her missing work was that I had to do TWO consults super fast for a couple of potential GAINSWave men (**GAINSWave is a non-invasive, painless therapy that uses sound waves to improve blood flow and rejuvenate erectile tissue**) between my pellet insertion patients. Neither started a care plan. By the way, I was too busy to record the consults, so I don't know what I did right or wrong. Then, the rep for Bio-T showed up late for lunch and got us 30 minutes behind in the afternoon. To top it off, the toilet broke in the women's bathroom, creating a mess. By the time I got home at 7 p.m., I had almost no time to eat dinner, and I spent 7:30–10:00 p.m. charting all the patients for the day."

I know that seems more than the average bad day in a medical clinic, but let's dig deeper and discover what really happened and also who is one hundred percent responsible for this super busy yet incredibly unproductive day. Hint: Her name starts with Amanda. Furthermore, the question, "Why were the stats not updated?" never got answered. We are in the weeds, and here, as Paul Harvey would say, is "The Rest of the Story."

For starters: the MA who left the supplies at the satellite on Friday should have been fired WAY before this drama unfolded. She had been given warnings and shown some downright bizarre behavior (she was finally canned about a month after being caught in the clinic sleeping at 3 a.m.). Amanda is an excellent provider. However, she lacked the leadership and confrontational skills to handle seriously troublesome employees. Unfortunately, these skills require some training and intention that most medical providers don't have time to learn.

Second: The PA was a half-in-half-out type of employee, meaning she was engaged in her role and patients for one minute and then super disengaged and isolated in her office with the door shut, probably checking Facebook and tiktok. The biggest challenge with her (and most midlevels from the hospital setting) is they feel like they know everything there is to know- so be super mindful of their coachability! When you are running a million-dollar practice where the production is based on medical providers performing services, they need to be all in, all the time. You will always get part-time results when you have part-time employees, guaranteed. I am not trying to bash them, but when your mid-levels are also moonlighting at the hospital or running another show, they WILL bring the attitudes and tone levels over from those other groups. It is just human nature. Speaking of which, this particular PA went back full-time to the hospital a few weeks after this scene played out.

Third: the MA should have been the one driving across town. Yes, Amanda lived in that area, but she was almost at the office when they realized the missing supplies. The MA does not drive production as an MD or mid-level can. Allowing the driver of the business to be offline is insanity.

Fourth: They should have bailed out and skipped the lunch meeting once the rep was late. Always have a backup plan for food if there is an in-service planned. These reps usually show up early and do their deal fast, but sometimes they get the office behind schedule. The provider or the office should dictate the time and how it affects their flow. If the rep is late, they should lose that time to keep everyone on schedule. The focus must stay on what produces the revenue and the patient experience.

Fifth: you should NEVER let anything get in the way of the two new consults. These are essential two-patient visits as new patients drive new revenue for the office. The office potentially lost thousands of dollars in revenue by not closing these patients. Remember, these two dudes will get their needs handled somewhere. If you run a Men's Health or ED clinic, you know how serious they are about addressing these issues. Once they make their minds up to get this situation handled, they are usually easy to close. I digress, back to Amanda's nightmare. The fact she didn't close them says a lot, and the fact she didn't record the conversation says even more. She was down in the weeds and fighting to get through the day.

Sixth: One major problem is that she could not complete her notes during work hours and had to finish them at home late in the evening. To avoid this, it is essential to simplify the note-taking process as much as possible. For cash-based services, consider using an EMR system and having the MA handle as much note-taking as possible. It is essential to avoid getting so busy that you end up doing notes at 10 p.m. – this is not a sustainable practice. Consider hiring an MA at $15 per hour to handle everyone.s note-taking.

Seventh (here is where things start to get interesting): please think about this for a moment a bit deeper. I am her consultant. She is paying me to spend time helping her make decisions based on her stats and the condition they are in and to identify the real problems that she is dealing with in the practice daily. What did we wind up spending most of our time on that Tuesday morning? Well, it was not what we should have been focusing our attention on, to be sure. We should have spent more time discussing marketing strategies, auditing her consults, and having crucial conversations and training we must have weekly. We had no stats to look at and analyze from the week before, and we had no recorded consults to audit. All we had was a massive pile of sh*t at the end of the day.

Perhaps it may be worth considering a different perspective when it comes to running a business. While owners and operators may have an intimate understanding of their operations, there are times when an outside perspective can be invaluable. This is where consultants come in. They can provide insights that may not have been considered before, and help identify areas that need improvement. Although consultants are compensated for their time, it is still up to the business owner to decide whether or not to act on their recommendations. It is important to be open to coaching, and willing to make the necessary changes to improve the business. After all, without change, there can be no progress. Ultimately, it is the business owner who must take responsibility for their own success and avoid getting stuck in a difficult situation. This is your business and you have to have the attitude you will do what is necessary to avoid standing in front of a huge pile of sh*t.

Back to Amanda. I had been actively trying to get her to move on from these two employees: The disengaged and uncoachable PA and the lunatic MA. However, a lot of times, this is much harder than it sounds. When I come into a new practice, I usually see an overwhelmed owner who, deep down, knows they have a problem employee, but they have either become too friendly with them, don't want the inconvenience of hiring and training someone else, or do not have the confrontational skills to make a change.

Before I move on to the ideal practice day, let's wrap a bow around this little Greek tragedy to clarify my point.

It's important to understand the consequences of not properly controlling a situation and being busy but not productive. This type of scenario happens frequently in various forms. The clinic is currently experiencing issues with a medical assistant who has personal problems, a physician assistant who is disengaged and only became accountable once held responsible. The clinic lost thousands in cash from two potential patients who ultimately went to a competitor down the street. The competitor will use this extra cash flow to ramp up their marketing and acquire more patients. The clinic's return on investment (ROI) will be skewed because they were unable to close the new patients that were brought in by the marketing efforts. In situations like this, clients tend to think that their marketing efforts are not working and stop investing in them. Losing two patients a week can result in losses of thousands in cash flow per month and hundreds of thousands of dollars in revenue per year. If each patient has a value of $5000, losing 2 per week comes up to $40,000.00 lost per month. That equates to half a million per year. This is serious cash flow potential. Without the cash flow for ads, the new patient numbers start to dwindle, and next thing you know, Amanda is broke and singing the Sunday Night Blues and close to deciding that moonlight for the lunatics at the hospital is her best option to get out of the nightmare scene SHE created.. It is a vicious cycle.

As for Amanda, she was busy on Monday, but the systems and staff broke down, making the day busy but not productive. This type of day is unsustainable, and eventually, something big will break. We see this type of scenario all the time. Luckily, Amanda survived and now has a thriving million-dollar-a-year practice, but it took some deep dives to get there. If any of this sounds familiar, please contact me.

Unfortunately, because we were busy addressing all of these issues, we were unable to focus on the training scheduled for that afternoon. To prevent this from happening, we need to establish systems and control mechanisms that allow us to handle challenges and train staff effectively. Otherwise, we risk spending all our time putting out fires instead of driving the clinic in the right direction

Amanda's Nightmare (Part 2)

I want to share another real-world example of your staff's importance and how one bad apple can affect your business and destroy your practice. Let me set the facts and the scene for this nightmare. Amanda had been using me as her consultant for six months, only a few months after her nightmare Monday story from above. Her clinic specialized in functional medicine/hormone replacement clinic. We had increased her collections from 25K a month to 90K on a bad month and 115K on a good one. On the surface, this sounds fantastic, but looking deeper, there were MAJOR problems under the hood. For starters, she had increased her payroll from 12k/month to 32k/month. Secondly, she has two covert antagonistic employees who are destroying her practice. She has become too friendly with them and was finding it very hard to let them go (fear-based decision-making).

This is how we found out the root of her problems. Remember, all of your problems come from either too few sales (cash flow), not enough profit (no system to pay yourself first or manage a budget), and/or operations issues (systems needing to be implemented correctly or not at all). To top it off, you may have all three, but when a scene like this plays out, you know you do.

This is how it went down. My client and the new office manager joined me on a Zoom meeting one Tuesday afternoon that lasted about four and a half hours. In this training, we slowly worked through numerous "bugs" in their systems, starting with recording the phones correctly and handling all inbound and outbound discovery calls. (A discovery call is the first conversation between a salesperson and a prospect who has expressed interest in a product or service. The call aims to determine if the prospect is a good fit for the business.) We then set up a new script to be used at the beginning and end of the calls to build trust and rapport with the clients. The next step was to create a role-play system to be practiced every week for 30 minutes. This included the instructions for correctly doing the system, which we will discuss later in the book. The next step is mapping out from each staff member what they hear and perceive as the most significant patient objections affecting the Sales Cycle.

Next, we focused on role-playing for the case manager, addressing how to handle the objections they hear, particularly money, time, stall tactics, etc. Then we worked on the history and exam part of the consultation for the provider. Finally, we established a follow-up plan for the patients who did not schedule at the end of the discovery call or did not close during the consultation. At the end of the Zoom call, I gave them until Friday to turn in the new scripts, objections they encountered, and the plan (just the plan) for starting the role-play training for the next week. Guess what happened?

Friday came and went. Crickets. I asked about it on Monday. Excuses. Wednesday, nothing. Friday, zilch. Another week went by. Three hundred thirty-six hours later (yes, I checked), we figured out the real problem. I finally contacted the office manager and confronted him with the fact that we needed that completed to start training. He was visibly frustrated and told me that not only did he not have any of it, but there was massive pushback from two staff members. There was also hesitancy from the new receptionist because she had been told they were committing HIPAA violations by recording phone calls. (This was not even close to accurate as we asked the potential new patient if it was okay to record the call before beginning). The staff members said they were too busy to train, so that was out. They were too busy even to set up our follow-up Zoom call.

Unfortunately, the inmates were running the asylum, and the owner was allowing it. These two staff members were doing things their way, and they knew their position was safe because they thought the owner could not replace them, even though owners always do. The office manager was pretty new, so the old guard was souring the receptionist and the owner. As a matter of fact, the same day, the owner came to me to complain that the new office manager was making mistakes and causing issues with the staff.

However, after working with the staff for some, I realized that they were not motivated to improve. They got paid regardless of their performance and were holding back the clinic without the owner's knowledge. This was concerning, and if they continued to refuse training or resist new ideas, they would have to be let go. Several other issues indicated that the staff was not open to change in this case.

It is a mind-blowing statistic, but 50% of all employees in this country merely put their time in at work and head home to watch the 86th season of The Bachelor or binge-watch reruns of Schitt's Creek. Twenty percent are downright counter-productive to their organizations. The average cost of bad employees to American businesses is roughly 500 billion dollars annually. Half a TRILLION dollars a year. A YEAR. Craziness. My third book will be on Leadership, and I will address this in detail.

Enough of the bedtime nightmares. They hit close to home and probably make you uncomfortable, so let's work on the ideal day. Let's focus on the solution to the dilemma of being productive versus being busy. Time to be more positive and productive (see what I did there)?

Game Day

It is time to map out what a day should look like as we piece everything together. We will go back through the book and work through these strategies with three big goals in mind:

1. Remember to enjoy the journey. After all, you're not on a 20-foot life raft floating in the Antarctic ocean.
2. Focus on the results, and don't just stare at a big pile of sh*t at the end of the day.
3. Remember to take extreme ownership of everything inside your office and be the absolute best team leader and visionary possible. This is YOUR company and vision.

"Success is your duty, obligation, and responsibility."
Grant Cardone

Having a solid morning routine to prepare for the day is a must. My most successful clients all have some form of meditation, exercise, journaling, or yoga practice before work to get their bodies and minds in a suitable space. I also recommend you have exercise and meditation as a morning routine.

The first thing you have to do to start the day is to ask yourself the self-assessment questions, but instead of yes or no, grade yourself mentally. To keep it simple, ask yourself these questions and rate them 1-5.

1. Am I walking the walk and being an effective leader?
2. Are you able to walk in your employees' shoes and look back on yourself through their eyes? Do you like what you see?
3. Can you do the exact same thing looking through your patients' eyes?
4. Are you thinking in an abundance or scarcity mentality?
5. Are you living in gratitude or materialism?

Ask yourself these questions on your car ride to the practice every morning. Use the time in the car to get your mind right for the day.

Show up early to the clinic. Small things like this count, and getting there ahead of the patients is critical. Remember that your staff is watching, and if you come in late, so will they. Guaranteed. If you don't get there early, you start your day behind and in a rush to catch up. It creates stress for everyone.

You should begin the day at the office with a staff meeting before the first patient is scheduled to arrive. The first staff meeting of the day is all about the stats for the day. I like to start the meeting by going around the room and having everyone say something they are grateful for today. Then, tell the staff how appreciative you are to have them help you save lives. You should then go through the schedule and work through their stats. The phone receptionist and front desk should present all of the new patients for the day and communicate to everyone anything that may be needed to ensure a positive first impression. The receptionist then has her audited checklists and score sheets for the new patients to be given to you for review. Any possible objections or upsets need to be addressed. Offer everyone as much praise as possible and keep the tone level as high as possible. This is not the time for a gripe session or to try to solve any operations problems.

No one should be eating breakfast or on their phones during this meeting. This meeting should be short and quick if everyone is prepared and focused.

As the first set of patients arrive for the morning hours, the staff should be on their stations, prepared, motivated, and ready to do their jobs. If you see patients yourself, you must be focused and prepared to work. If you are still seeing patients, consider stopping soon. It would be best if you were working to bring on other providers to replace yourself in the provider role. It is not that I don't want you seeing patients because you are too good to do it, but because you have the business to attend to. If you are not seeing patients, you can focus your attention on what is going on with the marketing, staff audits like the recording of the consults, and looking over the checklists turned in by the staff the prior day. You can focus on expanding the business or adding other profit centers. This will allow you to grow your empire. You seeing patients is the same as the CEO of Apple working in a store and trying to handle customer service issues daily. You can always cover if a provider is out, if one gets behind and needs help catching up that day, or if an influx of new patients needs to be scheduled quickly and there are not enough available slots. You can even have a few patient days per week, but you need time to focus on the practice, and it is difficult to grow a practice if you see a full load of patients. If you enjoy seeing patients and are unwilling to give up a full schedule of patients, you should be working to hire a CEO to run the business operations.

Noon hits with the understanding that lunch is not a time to eat a big meal. You consume a small, high-protein meal and catch up on your work, review stats, and handle any issues that need to be addressed. Take a short walk to clear and reset for the afternoon.

One day a week, lunch should be devoted to a weekly stats meeting. Give the staff a thirty-minute break and start the session. Schedule the training session for one hour. Bring lunch for the team so they can eat during the thirty-minute break, and it can start on time with no excuses. Every member should review their metrics and give the condition and action steps involved to improve them. This will help them understand how to use conditions to manage their position. If they learn to manage their position, eventually, it is less work for you. Your job then requires less oversight so that you can focus on other things. The meeting is again focused on production and metrics, nothing else. It should be done within 30 minutes.

The next thirty minutes of the meeting should be devoted to role-play and training, and you handle any operations issues. For example, the new phone receptionist scheduled a new patient consult for the PA or the MD but did not get them in at the right time. You do training on how to look at the schedule of both the providers and the case manager. Then, you role-play with them quickly using the system I detailed at the end of chapter two and practice how they handle that scene if it happens again. You do a brief role-play on the consult, produce to the provider, and scheduling the next appointment. You notice that the phone auditing scores aren't very high, so you spot-check the parts of the calls that need work and practice those. The case manager goes next and trains on being more mindful of the sales cycle and asking the hard questions.

1:30 comes, and the staff sees afternoon patients.

If you begin to use this system, you will notice that your office will become more efficient, and you can head home to be with the family or work on your passion projects instead of staying late every day to catch up or put out fires.

If you are gone in the afternoon, you should receive an email from the OM with the staff checklists around 5:30 p.m. If you are at the office, they should be turned in to you personally before anyone leaves. There are no exceptions. Staff login and input their stats before leaving.

One of the most critical aspects of the day is control. Are you in control of your day, or does it control you? The meetings at the beginning of the day provide structure. There are many reasons you do these, but one is to maintain control of the schedule and put yourself in a position to win that part of the clock. Even if you only control part of the day and place some order into the chaos, it is much better than spending all day putting out fires and playing catch up. Almost every problem can be solved through communication training and role-play, so do these meetings every day for sixty days and see what happens.

On your way home, go through the day and quickly ask yourself the same questions you asked on the way in.

Were you a good role model and leader? Did you treat all of the patients and staff with humble respect? Did your tone level and enthusiasm stay high?

Send me an email for a detailed map of how a work week should unfold. If you need help or are deficient in any of these areas, please reach out, and we can discuss how to move forward with one of the other firms I work with based on your specific needs. After helping over thirty clients in various fields outside of medicine, I can assure you that what you do is incredibly hard compared to most industries. You simply cannot do this on your own.

The weeks start rolling by, and month after month, year after year, they go by faster. Suddenly, you find yourself thirty years into your career in the same building, doing the same things in the same ways. If there is one piece of advice I can offer, it is that whatever you do moving forward, whether it is to start your practice, 10x the one you have, or sell out soon, please find a coach to help guide you on that journey. They have been in your shoes and can see your business - the good, bad, and ugly - from 30,000 feet and can help you make decisions without the emotions and reactions you would have. I used six different groups in my active practice days and learned and grew from every single one of them. Looking back, it was always worth the money, and investing in yourself should be where you spend the first dollars of every month.

Chapter 6

Mistake 6

Not having a Detailed Follow-Up System for Old Leads, Patients, and Video Testimonials.

FOLLOW UP MISTAKES

Amateurs versus Professionals

No doubt, not utilizing a systematic follow-up system alone costs you dearly. It is one of the easiest yet most neglected systems I see with my clients. We seem to get caught up in the new patient numbers and forget that our old patient database is full of people who still have healthcare issues and need our help. A follow-up system separates the amateurs from the professionals regarding the sales cycle. I fully admit that I was terrible at this system in active practice and running my own offices. However- I have seen clinics using follow-up as a significant marketing strategy, and the clinics generally collect an extra $18,000-$20,000 a month *in free money* (meaning it did not cost the clinic any extra cash flow to acquire the patient. That said, if you have a large patient database and are not doing anything with them or just ramped up some new service center, the ROI could be significantly higher. This is particularly true with high-end body contouring and laser aesthetics because of the high case fees. If you are new in practice, the reactivation system will be less critical, but the follow-up certainly will be.

That being said, let's play out a scene. I would like you to consider whether this has ever happened to you. Unfortunately, it happened to me on a damn near daily basis, and I was simply too busy and lazy at the same time to fix it.

- You spend a ton of money to make the phone ring.

- You have spent the time and money training a phone receptionist to handle the call correctly.
- You then have the new patient show up for the consultation and spend an hour realizing they are perfect candidates for the care you have to offer.
- At the end of the consultation, they tell you to take a hike and do not close.

Don't BS yourself; it happens to all of us. And it will continue to happen. The difference is in how you choose to respond.

Think about and write down the entire process of follow-up when a patient does not buy from you below:

_____

_____

_____

_____

_____

There are a million reasons why potential patients didn't close; truth be told, you may never find out why. However, with this system, you are guaranteed to capture at least a small percentage of the patients who did not close at the initial consultation.

Now, I would ask you to write down the follow-up sequence for when they DO buy from you:

_____

_____

_____

_____

_____

The most common mistakes I and many clients have made are listed below. Circle the ones that apply to your office:

Common Mistakes

1.   Not making any follow-up phone calls after the patient leaves.

Did you know the average sale on most financial transactions occurs around the 7th "touch" of follow-up? Granted, the patient will not come in seven times for a consultation (this is not like buying a car) however, calling them and asking if they had any questions, sending emails with a survey on what you and your staff could have done better, texting and asking for feedback on how to improve the patient experience in your practice, sending a handwritten letter once a month reminding them of your services and how much you miss them (the Simplify Group has a crazy cool machine that automates this part of the follow-up for you and it spits out a real handwritten letter with your signature. Email me for details.) Sending coupons or massive value-added deals, they may have missed will do nothing but significantly improve your overall business. These patients have already been to your office and would rather buy from the familiar than go down the street to an entirely new clinic unless your office did something negative and ran them off. My point to all this is - for crying out loud- do something with people who do not close. Even if they do not qualify for the services they came into your office for, use this opportunity to remind them of your other services and look for a second sale at every opportunity.

MAKE THE CALL. Do not stop at one touch—plan on reaching out at least ten different ways. And if you are short-staffed, outsource it to the call center. They can handle it for you.

2. You should consider using a Customer relationship management (CRM) system. Customer relationship management software is a set of integrated software solutions that help businesses track and manage customer relationships. There are numerous out there, and you just have to pick one. Spend the time learning the basics. These software are insanely crazy with all their integrations, bells, whistles, etc... Just learn the basics and then delegate it to someone on staff or turn it over to the Simplify group and let them dump their e-mails, texts, and handwritten letters into your system and automate it. The reason you must do this is

simple. It comes down to CONSISTENCY. You have to make the follow-up super simple and consistent to be effective.

3. Waiting too long to start the follow-up sequence. I highly recommend you get patients who do not close into a sequence with an immediate text message as soon as they leave that would go something like this: *"Mr. Jones, thank you so much for spending your valuable time in my office today. At the beginning of the consultation, I told you it would be my fault if I did not educate you well enough and give you all the options you needed to get started with our care plan, and I just wanted to say I am sorry. I loved meeting you and Mrs. Jones. If you have any questions or concerns, please text me at this number, and I will get back to you very soon."* I have never once received a text like this after a visit to a Doctor. I have been asked to leave a Google review (with the link to do it) from my dentist. I have gotten texts with my care plan schedule, which is standard these days, but I have never had a provider or case manager take ownership that they are the reason I am not starting the care I either needed or wanted.

4.   Always leave a message if they do not pick up on a call. This is branding 101. They need to hear your name and clinic name multiple times. Sooner or damn later, they will need your services, and if you are at the top of their mind, they will call you.

5.   Always 1. Listen to what the patient says about your office and any feedback they may have, and 2. Make sure to listen to see if they have any other needs your office may be able to deliver.

We have pre-made sequences for texts, emails, handwritten letters, and phone scripts. Just email me, and I will send you a free set. Just because they didn't sign up for care today does not mean they won't soon. It just means they are either shopping around, you screwed something up in the delivery of the consultation visit, or they have a specific buying style of always taking a week to decide on any financial lines. This one drives me crazy, but you will have this type of person come in on occasion. However, they legitimately may not have the money or the credit needed and simply need some time to figure out how to get the money. Or they have a legitimate objection of time, as in the case of a patient who will be on vacation and plans to begin care when they return. Again, whatever you do, please do not make my mistake and at least do the basics on the follow-up. There is just too much riding on your cash flow not to do this one system, especially considering you can automate it with Simplify and the call center. This one system is my biggest regret from my practice days. We averaged 28 new patients a week for years, and I was so damn busy with the new patient consults I just got super lazy with this system, and I am certain it cost me millions. Please do not make the same mistake I did.

Example of what the follow-up sequence should look like when they do not buy:

- Immediate text message with apology and or thank you
- 10 more text messages over the next thirty days.
- 10 emails with embedded links to testimonials and before and after pics. Use material from the demo.
- 4 handwritten letters to be delivered over the next three months.
- Birthday cards.
- Phone calls every 30 days to check in and see how they are doing. Do not stop until they tell you to quit calling, die, or come in and buy.

Example of what a follow process should look like after they DO buy:

- A group family picture with the staff welcoming the patient into your family.
- Walking them to their car and opening the door for them.
- Personally calling them that night to see how they are doing and if they have any questions.
- A 10-deep email campaign with testimonials and embedded before and after pictures.
- A text message one week into care asking for a Google review. You may want to wait until you hear the patient say they are feeling better, losing weight/looking younger, and then ask for the review.
- A system in place after a certain number of visits or periods of time to ask them for a referral. See above for that system.

Conclusion

My mission is to cure medical provider poverty. That is my mission statement. When I decided to write this book, my only real goal was to provide five or six nuggets that others could take along and start implementing in their practices immediately. I skipped numerous other topics because I simply could not write them all up. Running a practice is not easy, and there are always challenges. If it were easy- everyone would be doing it well and living an amazing life in abundance. Unfortunately, way more often than not, this is not the case. Providers in all fields struggle to run and operate their businesses simply because they have not been taught how to do it.

Finding good people and keeping staff are the biggest problems for owners by far. Patients are more educated and more demanding than ever. Regulations and compliance are difficult to maintain, and the rules constantly change. With that being said, being a medical provider, changing the lives of our patients, and helping them regain their health is a gratifying profession. I hope this book can serve as a basic guide to help you navigate some of the aspects of being an owner-operator. I hope it sets you on the right path toward abundance in your life and allows you to chase your passion. If all you got was one solid piece of data or a good system to implement, then the book was a success.

As a quick summary, Please start with system number 1, the phones, and fix those as fast as possible. Then, train on the sales cycle and make it your number one priority. Learn to properly role-play and implement it into a consistent training program. Record and audit the consults. DO THIS RIGHT NOW. Your financial life depends on it. Map out your marketing. Get the entire quarter mapped out and use the sales event strategy. Take that massive action. It will change your life. Use your old lists. Market like hell to them. They still need your services! Hold your staff accountable for their statistics. You are not giving out a participation trophy to your organization's crummy, entitled performers. Nothing changes when nothing changes..... Plan your day and do whatever is necessary to stay on point. You can always make more money but never get wasted time back. Let's GOOOO! Imagine I just said all that to you in a Rick Flair voice. I work with numerous other consultants in Regenerative and Physical Medicine, Weight Loss, Men's Health, and Aesthetics spaces. I cannot stress enough how important it is for you to have one. You need help and a guide who can help you get the most out of your practice and life. If you need assistance finding the right fit for your group, please email drben@regenmedicalconsulting.com, and we can discuss how you can move forward. Also, please email me with any questions, and feel free to reach out with any feedback or thoughts. I am here to help. Thank you for sticking through the book, and I hope it has helped you with at least a couple of strategies you can implement this week to increase your revenue and help you manage the practice.

I look forward to hearing from you soon!!

Appendix A

They say the average CEO reads a business book a month. To be honest, I average about 25 books every year and I also read numerous books at one time. The usual theme is I get into one and they use source material from another book and then I am off to dig into that book if the topic is more relevant to my current situation. This list is just designed as a start. I am also adding in the list of consultants. Some in but mostly out of the medical space. Business owners need a coach no matter game they are playing so I am adding in the groups I know do a great job and will help if you decide to use them instead of my group. Some of them have better tools and others are specific for certain needs like the Profit First guys. As the owner you decide who you use as your guide- I promise it will show up in better results, patient satisfaction and a better looking P& L and cash flow statement at the end of the month.

Books
1. The EOS life and How to be a Great Boss by Gino Wickman- just buy every book this guy and his partners have written. They are ballers.
2. Profit First, Fix This Next and The Pumpkin Plan by Mike Michaelowicz
3. Ready Aim Fire by Micheal Masterson
4. If You're Not First You're Last by Grant Cardone.
5. Emotional Success for Sales Success by Colleen Stanley
6. The Diamond Cutter by Geshe Michael Roach.
7. How to Win Friends and Influence People by Dale Carnegie - again- just all his materials.
8. Built to Last and Good to Great by Jim Collins.
9. The Truth About Taxes by Sean Briscombe.
10. Scaling Up by Verne Harnish, Spencer Cannon and Crew.
11. Mastering the Rockefeller Habits again by Verne Harnish.

12. The Power of Discipline by Daniel Walter
13. Atomic Habits by James Clear.
14. Grit by Angela Duckworth.
15. The Work by Byron Katie- This one book will do more for your headspace than just about anything else.
16. Dare to Lead by Brene Brown.
17. The 21 Irrefutable Laws of Leadership by John Maxwell.
18. The Subtle Art of Not Giving a Fu*k by Mark Manson.

Consultants and Coaches I would hire without reservation.

1. Dave Anderson (Leadership).
2. John Maxwell (Leadership).
3. Mike Michaelowicz and his posse'.
4. Verne Harnish and his gang at Scalingup.com. He also works with Mike.
5. Blue IQ and the Frogley brothers if you are a Chiro or Dentist.
6. DCI and the Seeds of True Success - This is a **MUST** and is outside of any consulting so even

when you hire a different group or myself - you have to spend some time training with this group. It will blow you away.
7. The Silva Method with Jose Silva. Crazy good program.

No matter how good your consultant is, the only person who is going to change your practice is you. Period. Start with these books and ALWAYS keep learning.

Appendix B

Chapter 2: The Sales Cycle. The graphs came directly out of Grant Cardone's " The Sales Execution Workbook" by Grant Cardone. I highly recommend his University platform to train your staff and also recommend this particular training for medical providers.

Chapter 4: Stats. The training on this system for stats (KPI's) came out of an old school book called *Breaking the Code: The Mysteries of Modern Management Unlocked* by Ravenwood Management. This book is fantastic for the newbie in practice and has several basic fundamental systems that can help fill the gap for new providers who have just started in the business world.

About the Author

Dr. Ben Barton D.C. is the founder and CEO of Regen Medical Consulting and an alumnus of Appalachian State University and Palmer College of Chiropractic. With over 20 years of experience owning and operating multiple practices across South Carolina, Dr. Barton started RMC in the summer of 2020 during Covid. Dr. Barton has generated over 23 million dollars in sales during his career and has helped close to 100 Owners/Providers in the Physical Medicine, Aesthetics, and Men's Health space achieve success at a very high level.

He lives in Charleston, SC, with his better half, Heather, and insane dog Bella. His hobbies include extreme mountaineering, and he is working towards his goal of hiking the Seven Summits by his fifty-fifth birthday. 2 down, 5 to go.

Dr. Barton also spends several hours weekly in the recovery space, including conducting weekly meetings with Palmetto Behavioral Health. He has sponsored close to 30 men in their recovery and is passionate about continuing his path of recovery by helping others.

Made in the USA
Columbia, SC
11 October 2023